INSIDE
THE ORCHESTRA

BOOKS BY ALAN JEFFERSON

The Operas of Richard Strauss in Great Britain 1963
The Leider of Richard Strauss 1971
Delius (Master Musicians) 1972
The Life of Richard Strauss 1973

INSIDE
THE ORCHESTRA

Alan Jefferson

KEITH REID LTD SHALDON DEVON

ISBN 0904094 04 9

Printed in Great Britain by
W & J Mackay Limited, Chatham

For Keith Reid Ltd
Shaldon, Devon

For R.G., H.B. and C.T.,
three of the best

Music is a rum go . . .
Philip Heseltine

Do you really think these people want to
learn and make progress? They only regard
their occupation as a milch-cow.
Gustav Mahler (on orchestral players)

CONTENTS

	LIST OF ILLUSTRATIONS	9
	FOREWORD	11
1	ANATOMY OF THE ORCHESTRA	15
2	STRINGS	31
3	WOODWIND	44
4	HORNS AND BRASS	63
5	TIMPANI, PERCUSSION AND KEYBOARD INSTRUMENTS	74
6	CONDUCTORS	87
7	MANAGEMENT	107
8	BBC ORCHESTRAS	128
9	MAIN BRITISH ORCHESTRAS	142
10	MAIN EUROPEAN AND AMERICAN ORCHESTRAS	152
	POSTSCRIPT	161

APPENDICES:

TRILINGUAL NAMES OF ORCHESTRAL INSTRUMENTS	162
ORCHESTRAL LAYOUTS	163
INSTRUMENTAL AND VOCAL COMPASSES	166

GLOSSARY OF TERMS	167
SELECT READING LIST	176
INDEX	177

LIST OF ILLUSTRATIONS

PHOTOGRAPHS   FACING
The string quartet: 1st and 2nd violins, viola, cello   48
The bass: normal bow hold, Dragonetti hold, and pizzicato   48
Woodwind: flute, oboe, clarinet (E♭ and B♭)   49
Woodwind: bassoon and contrabassoon   49
Brass: horn, trumpet, trombone, tuba, euphonium   64
Brass: cymbals and timpani   64
Percussion: triangle, tubular bells, tam-tam, bass drum   65
Percussion: vibraphone, celeste, xylophone, glockenspiel   65
Four musical knights: Sir Henry Wood, Sir Adrian Boult,
    Sir Thomas Beecham, Bt, Sir Malcolm Sargent (*courtesy
    BBC*)   96
Four great European Conductors: Arturo Toscanini, Wil-
    helm Furtwängler, Sir Georg Solti (*courtesy Decca*),
    Herbert von Karajan (*courtesy Polydor*)   97
Rehearsal for a broadcast under Pierre Boulez (*courtesy
    BBC*)   112
Concert at the Royal Festival Hall, London (*courtesy RFH*)   112
Promenade Concert Last Night (*courtesy BBC*)   113

FIGURES
Full orchestral score showing normal order of main instru-
    ments (*courtesy Messrs Boosey & Hawkes*)   25
Orchestral score illustrating the piano as an accompanying
    instrument (*courtesy Messrs Boosey & Hawkes*)   27
Harmonic series based on G   28
Orchestral layout of 1784 (*courtesy OUP*)   38
Six bars from an orchestral score showing rational nota-
    tion as in a Penguin score (*courtesy Penguin Books*)   52
The same six bars notated normally   53
Mouthpieces of horn and trumpet in section and half true
    size   66
Extract from a timpani part showing many bars' rest   75

Extract from the bass drum and cymbal part in Brahms's
Academic Festival Overture   76
Full score divided into two systems and showing the piano
part as semi-percussive   85
Wagner's layout of the orchestra in 1845 (*courtesy OUP*)   163
Layout of the New York Philharmonic Society Orchestra
in 1897 (*courtesy OUP*)   163
Frequent twentieth-century layout of the orchestra in
London (*courtesy OUP*)   164
Layout of the orchestra as favoured by Leopold Stokowski   165
Orchestral and vocal compasses (*courtesy Victor Gollancz
Ltd*)   166

FOREWORD

THE PURPOSE OF THIS BOOK IS TO INTEREST AND INFORM not only those who want to make music their career, but also many members of concert audiences who wish to know more about the mysteries of orchestras and what makes them tick. Hence the title of the book, *Inside the Orchestra*. What lies inside it is revealed here in an effort to show that being an orchestral musician is both highly rewarding and beset with problems. This is not done maliciously, but to try and give a fairer picture of life in an orchestra than has ever been shown in the past in adulatory and complacent descriptions by authors who prefer to portray Heaven without Hell. As you know, these are usually complementary.

So forgive me, music students, music graduates, musicians too, if I have been unduly repetitive in matters of common knowledge to us, or too concise in the instrumental sections. These are for the inquiring lay reader, although some of the anecdotes will be new to everybody.

For those who pick up this book to read it with a view to joining the profession, or even to entering orchestral management, I would strongly suggest that you go to your music school, pass out of it, and then if possible go to university and learn about life. If you don't manage to go to university, learn about life some other way before you join an orchestra. Once your instrumental technique has been acquired you will need only to keep it sharpened up: you will never lose it irreparably. Then follow the musical press and apply to be auditioned for any orchestra at all. Get in. Don't be too choosey. If it is not a very good orchestra, it doesn't matter, in fact you will show up to greater advantage, and when you move you will have got definite, practical, living experience to wave at your next audition. And when you are accepted into the orchestra of your choice you will be a fully-rounded person with this experience behind you. You cannot help being an asset to them, while you

11

can see them all more clearly because you will be mentally older than all those who have gone from the nursery to school to music school to orchestra—protection all the way.

ACKNOWLEDGEMENTS

I AM INDEBTED TO MANY PEOPLE, SOME OF WHOM I DON'T even know, who were willing to be consulted and then gave their advice and help. I wish to express my special gratitude to Robert Threlfall for reading the typescript and making valuable comments; to Ronald Gilks and Charles Thomas for having put themselves out on my behalf; and to the Managements of the following orchestras for having supplied me with facts about their conductors:

City of Birmingham Symphony Orchestra
Boston Symphony Orchestra
Bournemouth Symphony Orchestra
Chicago Symphony Orchestra
Cincinnatti Symphony Orchestra
Concertgebouw Orchestra of Amsterdam
Hallé Orchestra
Leipzig Gewandhaus Orchestra
Royal Liverpool Philharmonic Orchestra
Scottish National Orchestra

I must also thank the following music publishers for permission to reprint score-pages:

Boosey & Hawkes Ltd, London
Penguin Books Ltd, London

and the organisations listed on pages 9–10 for permission to reproduce the photographs.

ALAN JEFFERSON
Guildford, Surrey
November 1973

1

ANATOMY
OF THE ORCHESTRA

IMAGINE YOURSELF TO BE A YOUNG VIOLINIST, WELL
trained at one of the Schools of Music, who has been engaged
this morning as a deputy to fill the position of a member of a
London orchestra who has been taken ill with 'flu. You have
been suddenly told to go along to the Royal Festival Hall in
London for a morning rehearsal and also for the evening performance. It is getting on for ten o'clock on a cold November
morning as you come out of the Waterloo underground, turn
left under Hungerford Bridge, and force your way against the
north wind and sleet, beating at you from across the river. You
make for the Artists' Entrance with head down.

There, in the warmth and dry of his sanctum, Fred or Bert,
depending who's on duty, will look at you through the glass,
note the fiddle-case under your arm, nod at you in an off-hand
sort of a way, and then cease to have any further interest in you.
He will know that you are turning left through the glass door
towards the lift, that architect's afterthought in an otherwise
well-planned building.

Several other people are grouped round the lift, obviously
musicians, and you realise that you don't know any of them, not
even by sight. So you stand a little away from them, though not
out of earshot. It always means waiting for the lift here. The
ground floor is called '1' and the lift has five floors to negotiate
and is slow. Some of the Hall's management personnel have
been taken to the top. One musician is addressing the others:
'. . . and it came in fourth, so I lost the lot. After all that. I ask
you. But tell you what, I've got the winner for Tuesday, 2.30.
And I'm not giving it to any of you lot either, not even you,
mate!' Much laughter.

You may freeze. Racing talk before a concert like this? How

15

mundane. Why aren't they discussing the Brahms Violin Concerto or the Mahler Symphony? Or the conductor of the programme? But hardened musicians are seldom found discussing their work short of asking 'What's on the stand?' Nor the work for any other day either. Generally speaking they aren't interested; they don't regard music in the same, intellectual way as you do, because most of them will have seen, heard and done it all many times before, and the novelty wore off long ago. The fact that the variety of ways in which they had been asked to play a standard work may have made interesting comparisons, passes them by: it is just another fool conductor changing the markings so as to be different.

Very likely they are standing there, running down tonight's conductor, that great man you cannot yet believe you will be playing for; or they are voicing their opinions of the soloist, expressing their views on his new instrument, perhaps an Amati, bought in America for $40,000. (Featured in the magazine, *The Strad*.)

At last the lift arrives and we go up to the third floor, noticing what a long time it takes between the second and third, half the height of the building. When the lift doors open and we spill out, we arrive in the middle of complete pandemonium. Nearly a hundred musicians are milling about within the small confines of two corridors and the area in and about the lift which includes the artists' bar, not yet open. Julie, the barmaid, always was late, seeing her 'mother in hospital' at all hours of the day and night. The second corridor, the broad one immediately behind the concert platform has comfortable seats all down one side on which are now to be found fiddle-cases, coats, hats and a variety of coloured scarves.

Then one voice makes itself heard above all the rest. The personnel manager is calling out: 'Come along now, please. Come ALONG everybody. It's almost ten o'clock. It's time you were on.'

The players don't react at all like soldiers at such a command. (So few of them were real ones.) They just amble on, taking their own time, still talking, still smoking although it is definitely a NO SMOKING auditorium. The personnel manager flashes past, still shouting, and notices you. It's his job to notice everybody. 'Oh yes,' he says, 'thanks for coming at such short notice.

You're on the back desk of the seconds, with Mr Williams—
Jack Williams. D'you know him?' And without waiting for a
reply, he's off again. 'Come along please, PLEASE!' as if his
lungs are going to burst.

You follow the crowd and step through the light green cur-
tain, to where three thousand empty seats are staring at you and
looking very close, as if they have never seen you before and
wonder what you are doing there. Shaking yourself from a
momentary mesmerism, you are aware of the sound of the
orchestra tuning up, that inimitable cacophony which is always
so exciting. You find your seat, greet Jack Williams, and tune
up yourself.

The orchestra's leader stands up, points his bow at the first
oboe, and tucks his violin under his chin as he sits down. Instantly, and for the first time, there is a sort of discipline as the
oboe's *A* cuts through the incoherent web of orchestral sound
and collects it all round it. All instruments gather, as it were,
to a single point of sound, like iron filings to a magnet, and there
is nothing to be heard but a great big open *A* that fills the whole
hall, and stretches from bottom to top of the orchestra's compass as every instrument obeys the oboe's call to order. This
all-enveloping *A* is enriched by the common chord played as an
arpeggio, and then the whole musical machine quietens down,
adjusts itself, shakes itself out and is ready to begin.

The conductor walks on, smiling and confident. He shakes the
leader's hand as he passes him and mounts the rostrum. If he is
brand new to them, or popular with the orchestra, the string
players tap their music stands with their bows and the other
players either shuffle or stamp their feet. If the conductor is held
in low esteem or is little known, or is downright unpopular,
there is complete silence, save perhaps for a brass instrumental
noise (in badly behaved orchestras) that has only one interpretation.

This morning, however, they like him, and so we are off to a
good start. As he knows his job, this conductor does not waste
time with words of greeting, strained jokes, or unimportant
chat. He gets on with it and says: 'Good morning, gentlemen.
This is to be the procedure today. I shall be taking the overture
first, then the concerto. The soloist will be with us half an hour
before the break. After the break the symphony; but as we

worked so hard on it yesterday, I don't anticipate keeping you here until much after 12.30.' (More, and prolonged stamping and the odd cheer.) 'So now, anybody not needed in the overture . . .' He does not need to finish because they are half-way out already. The conductor waits a moment longer and continues: 'The overture then? Right?' He looks at the leader who nods, the conductor has already raised his arms, and his downbeat signifies the start of (almost) three hours of rehearsal.

What are the ingredients which make the sometimes frightening, sometimes deeply moving, mostly stirring group of people and instruments who are the originators of all the sounds that we go to hear, in an orchestra?

Suppose that we start at the beginning, by explaining the conventional groups of instruments which can be seen and heard at any concert that includes works by composers between Mozart and Brahms, that is to say from about 1750 to 1900. Musical instruments are played in one of three ways: they are either scraped, blown or banged. But these rough words are generally used disparagingly, for while they are true, they give no impression of the results achieved when the instruments are in the hands of trained musicians. The following table shows all the common, and also some less common instruments in the three categories. There are four 'departments'—the woodwind, brass, percussion and strings. Each department is divided into sections, a section consisting of similar instruments whose players sit together in the orchestra.

The table also shows the order of appearance of all the instruments in a score, although there is none, so far as I know, in which all of them occur together. The instruments within each section appear in descending order of compass, the highest pitched instruments above the lower. Where there are voices in the work, they come between keyboard instruments and the strings, with solo voices above any chorus or choruses. Similarly, a solo instrument's line is written above those of the other instruments in the department.

The woodwind department contains the greatest variety of instruments. Don't be surprised if you see a flautist playing on a silver instrument and not a wooden one, for the silver flute is still part of the woodwind! And if you see a clarinettist putting his instrument down and picking up another of a different shape

TABLE 1

	Departments	Sections
THESE INSTRU-MENTS ARE BLOWN	WOOD-WIND	FLUTES Piccolo Flute Alto flute OBOES Oboe Oboe d'amore Cor anglais Heckelphone Sarrusophone CLARINETS E♭ D B♭ A Basset-horn Bass SAXOPHONES Soprano, alto, tenor, bass BASSOONS Bassoon Contra-bassoon
THESE INSTRU-MENTS ARE BLOWN	BRASS	FRENCH HORNS Horn in F (or double horn in F/B♭) Wagner tuba TRUMPETS Trumpet Cornet Flugelhorn TROMBONES Tenor Bass Bass trumpet TUBAS Euphonium Bass tuba (Sousaphone)

	Departments	*Sections*

THESE INSTRU-MENTS ARE BANGED	PER-CUSSION	TIMPANI
		PERCUSSION
		    many different instruments
		KEYBOARD
		    Celeste
		    Harmonium
		    Piano
		    Organ
		HARP

THESE INSTRU-MENTS ARE SCRAPED	STRINGS	VIOLINS VIOLAS CELLOS DOUBLE BASSES

altogether, with a wide mouth, and probably of silver- and gold-plated appearance, it will be a saxophone (which has the same fingering), and you may very well be listening to Gershwin or Bernstein. Horns form a connection between the woodwind and the brass in that they can be made to sound gentle. Although they can also be made to sound strident, they are not as piercingly powerful as trumpets or trombones. The horns do not generally wish to be associated with the rest of the brass and regard themselves as rather special.

Although there are a great number of compositions for the strings alone, that is to say, for a string orchestra, there is little music written for the orchestral wind sections alone—Gustav Holst comes to mind here. Music for woodwind alone is generally classified as chamber music and is played by a wind ensemble, so need not concern us here.

But when it comes to the brass instruments there is a lot of music for them—some people think far too much—and the brass band world has its own types of instruments that are played by amateurs and not by professionals.

The percussion instruments occupy a fascinating and immensely interesting department of the orchestra (sometimes known as the 'kitchen department'), not only because they are the oldest of all musical instruments, but because the players generally move about between them and are not anchored throughout the concert to one chair as all the other players are. The piano and harp are in this section as well; the piano used in this instance percussively and not in a soloistic capacity; and the harp, its relative, which is struck with the hands as its strings are plucked with the fingers. Richard Strauss, for example, in his operas *Ariadne auf Naxos* and *Intermezzo* uses the piano both melodically and percussively; Stravinsky uses it to almost its fullest stretch in *Petrouchka* and *The Firebird*, and very percussively indeed in a third ballet, *Les Noces*.

The string department is, without doubt the most important of all the departments in the orchestra. There are wind bands and military bands and brass bands which do not use strings at all (except possibly one 'rhythm' bass), but an orchestra could not do without them. The leader of the orchestra is a string player, as we know, and it is he and his section, the first violins, who are the leading section for almost the whole time. The second violins, under their own principal, are closely related to the firsts, whether they sit adjacently or opposite each other across the orchestra, depending upon how the conductor likes them to be placed. The violas, the cellos and the double basses are all supporting sections in making up the four-part harmony required, so that the total number of string players may well represent half the orchestra's strength. Despite their great importance, musically, they can all, at any one time, easily be drowned by the wind and percussion. One can say that an orchestra is no better than its least good string player, and that the combined forces of the strings, if they are really good, can determine the virtuoso nature of the whole orchestral instrument. For a high standard of wind and percussion playing is moderately easy to come by; a superb standard of string playing is not.

Each of the departments of the orchestra is explained more fully in the following chapters.

It is odd that one does not often find people from one department of the orchestra who spend a lot of time with others from a different department, except for reasons of physical attraction. A violinist will hardly ever be seen with a tuba player, and it is exceptional for a flautist to be married to a cellist, although I happen to know two such players who are happily married. The combination of cellist and bass or flautist and oboist is far more likely. Percussion players will always be found together for the simple reason that their talk is likely to be about their instruments, so by the groups of instrumentalists being segregated musically as well as socially, they all understand each other far better, though only within their narrow limits. There are players who have been with the same colleagues in the same orchestra for years and know each other only by their Christian- or nick-names because they never have cause to talk to each other for long, being in far-flung sections. One oboist who goes on remorselessly about his reeds and reed-making to a group of string players will not be understood nor be found in the least inspiring. The latter will far prefer to discuss the merits of new nylon strings, resin, or the rising cost of good bows. Why anybody has to blow down one of those pipes, they all agree, is beyond them. So messy. And as for those gross brass instruments like the trombone and the horns, some of them even have taps to let out the saliva on to the floor. Quite disgusting. There is, after all, they say, nothing so neat, so refined and so delicate as the violin.

Of course all the players in an orchestra must live together once they start to play. In fact they have a healthy respect for one another and seldom hesitate, during rehearsal, to applaud a colleague who has given a good solo, or to accord the usual stamping for the very opposite reason. This is not so much in derision as in a good-natured expression of understanding that it can happen to anyone. Should the player in an exposed position continue to go wrong, however, there is silence as in the case of the unpopular conductor, and the player will be expected to apologise to the conductor afterwards—*not* at the time.

It may already be evident that most sections of the orchestra within each department are made up of four groups of instruments. This is because since 1600 a 'complete' harmony has depended upon four parts, or voices, whether of human throats or from instruments. It does not follow that by altering the number of instruments in a section, their weight of sound will be correspondingly altered when compared with the other instruments in the whole orchestra. In certain cases a change of balance is not discernible, in others the result may be disastrous. Instrumental balance is a very delicate and sensitive matter and one which every conductor has at the forefront of his consciousness. The following table gives some idea of four fairly conventional orchestral arrangements of instruments:

		A	B	C	D
Woodwind	Flutes (2nd doubles piccolo)	3	3	2	2
	Oboes (2nd doubles cor anglais)	3	3	2	2
	Clarinets (2nd doubles bass or E♭ clar.)	3	3	2	[2]
	Bassoons (2nd doubles contra when there are three)	3	2	2	2
Horns	(In 1800 only 2 horns. Later in larger orchs, 4. Even a 5th or 'bumper' to relieve the first)	4(+1)	4	4	2
Brass	Trumpets	3 or 4	3	2	2 or 1
	Trombones (2 tenor 1 bass, except in France where 3 tenors)	3	3	3	—
	Tuba (with or below bass trombone)	1	1	(1)	—
Others	Timpani (4, or more usually 3 timps tuned differently and played by one person)	1	1	1	1
	Percussion (the number of players usually varies from 1–3 depending on demands)	1–3	1–3	1–2	
	Harp (extension of percussion)	1–2	1	1	—
Strings	1st Violins	16	14	10	8
	2nd Violins	14	12	8	6
	Violas	12	10	6	4
	Cellos	10	8	6	4
	Basses	8	6	4	2

The instrumentation shown under A describes number of players needed to fulfil the demands of works by the nineteenth-century romantic composers such as Bruckner, Mahler, Wagner and, later, those of Richard Strauss, though even more instruments than these may well be needed, making it nearer to 100 players than 90.

Instrumentation B is as for Brahms and for other romantic compositions that are more modest in their demands. Instrumentation C is for a medium-sized orchestra, able to play almost anything in the standard eighteenth–twentieth-century repertoire outside 'giant' demands. And finally instrumentation D is for an orchestra of Haydn's, Mozart's and Beethoven's times, during which the clarinets appeared for the first time, so are shown in brackets for pre-1700.

You will see by how much the strings outweigh in numbers the remaining instruments in each classification, yet when discussing a composition, it will be referred to by musicians as needing, for example, 'triple woodwind'. This implies that the number of woodwind instruments govern the number of strings and brass to be used. This works well for all practical purposes, although certainly not in the way which the composer originally conceived the balance. It merely acts as a guide to the forces that will be required.

An orchestral score (see Fig. 1, p. 25) is normally laid out in a conventional way no matter what the nationality of the composer. With small changes of instruments there has been little variation in scores over the last 150 years, but before that one could sometimes find the strings at the top. Nowadays, and reading from top to bottom, the piccolos, which can play the highest notes, come first, while the contra bassoon, which plays the lowest in the woodwind section, has its part printed on the last line of this section. This follows through the brass (trumpet to tuba) and in the percussion, to the strings at the foot of the page (violin to double bass). The number of players in each section is sometimes shown at the front of a score, with any special instructions that the composer may have, but this is not always the case. It certainly helps when one wants to extract the exact numbers in each section and set them down.

There is a way of indicating the instrumental forces in a composition without laboriously writing down all the names of the instruments. Taking their order in score order, if there are three each of flutes, oboes and clarinets and bassoons, they are shown as 3.3.3.3. Should there, for instance, be no oboes and only one

Fig. 1. Page of full orchestral score showing normal order of main instruments

bassoon, it would then read 3.0.3.1. In the case of column A in Table 2, it would read, in this abbreviated form:

3.3.3.3., 4.3.3.1., 3 perc., hp, str.

'hp' means harp, and 'str' is strings. (3 perc. includes 1 timp. and 2 perc.) The strings are seldom itemised. This form is useful for music catalogues, and for the orchestral notice board, but is not to be found in the score. If any unusual instruments (like bass oboe) are needed, they will be specified. But percussion is not enlarged upon and it will be necessary for the principal player to look at the score and work it out as to how many players are going to be required.

The page from Richard Strauss's full score of *Ariadne auf Naxos* (see Fig. 2, p. 27) shows a somewhat unusual combination of instruments in which there is a voice, a harmonium, a piano and two harps all going with a chamber orchestra (double woodwind).

In the glossary you will find a list of the names of the instruments most commonly found in scores, together with their German and Italian equivalents.

The number of instruments required in a composition is specified by the composer, but may be altered either by the conductor or by financial dictates in an 'arrangement', or, we hope, will be given with the full number. Sometimes the composer has made an alternative version of the work which he has authorised for a lesser number of instruments, or else some other person has done this with or without his knowledge and approval. Musicians are often unhappy about playing a work with reduced instrumentation simply because it does not allow their particular section to be at the right strength (this applies to large string forces and to wind instruments). The reason they will give will be the altruistic one that it is not what the composer originally wished.

The other chief alteration or change in an orchestra's ways is in the placing of the groups of instruments in relation to each other. The Appendix on pages 163–165 shows some characteristic ways of placing the instruments in an orchestra, but these are by no means the only ones because quite often its arrangement is dictated by the shape of the platform or other area available. Certain conductors have their own foibles, such as

Fig. 2. Page of orchestral score illustrating the piano as an accompanying instrument

Stokowski, who likes twelve double basses all strung out in a line along the back even behind the timpani and percussion.

Yet these variants in seating are not very great, and the leader is always in the same position on the conductor's left; the four woodwind principals (flute, oboe, clarinet and bassoon) must sit in a square to get complete consolidation of hearing and of sound among themselves; and the weightier brass instruments and the timpani and percussion tend to be at the back, or else they drown the sound of the strings and the woodwind.

At this juncture we should explain what musical sounds are made of, which is by no means straightforward. Pure musical

Fig. 3. The harmonic series based on **G**

tones are uninteresting, and have little use in the orchestral texture. They are to be most clearly found in wide-stopped organ pipes, but not in reed-pipes. For reed-pipes in organs and all orchestral instruments obey what is called the harmonic series function. The tones are embellished with *harmonics* which add brilliance and brightness to the sound. These harmonics are a fixed series of other notes which sound when the basic or *fundamental* note is struck or blown and, in fact, go on indefinitely upwards, getting fainter and fainter. Nobody, unless he listens very carefully, is probably aware of harmonics, and this unalterably fixed progression is shown above. The ratio is: octave, fifth, major fourth, major third, minor third, reduced minor third (because the B♭ shown in brackets is flatter than indicated), major second, etc. It must be stressed that many of these intervals do not correspond exactly to the notes as tuned in modern scales, and cannot be reproduced for example on a well-tempered piano. However, the object is not to reproduce these notes, because they happen as a matter of course, but merely to indicate how the series is related to its fundamental, and by which means a bloom is put over this fundamental so that it glows richly.

Strictly speaking the word *note* signifies the complete sound with its family of harmonics (or upper partials as they are sometimes called); the word *tone* merely the sound from a simple vibration without the harmonics. In common parlance this differentiation is not observed, and the true, acoustical sense of the two words has been distorted.

Nor does this apply only to lower notes, as the bass G shown in the example as fundamental. Because the interval between the 1st and 2nd, 2nd and 3rd, 3rd and 4th are wider than the successive notes in the harmonic series, they are illustrated in this way to avoid leger lines. But even a fundamental above the treble stave will observe the same pattern of harmonics, too high for the human ear to appreciate, but nevertheless giving a bloom in the same manner.

It must now appear that an orchestra, of whatever size, is a highly organised body, not only organised but disciplined by natural forces as well as by human ones. If you hear an orchestra tuning up before a rehearsal or a concert and notice that the manager or the leader is not able to obtain instant silence, you might think them very undisciplined. But no. They save the almost military precision which is needed until just before playing, so that they can perfect their tuning and get themselves quite ready to produce the best possible results. And yet there are always individuals who like to carry on warbling in an extrovert manner, for each one is desperately in love with the sound of his own instrument.

Playing in an orchestra requires a special kind of technique which comes only from experience in doing it, nor does this technique, once gained, stop there. I know a clarinettist who says he still learns new ways of playing; of covering mistakes, defects or slips by himself and others; of getting round difficult passages in new ways—all this after twenty years in the same seat. This is indeed progression, for this admirable man knows he will never be an acknowledged soloist, yet continues to perfect his art within the framework in which he works. It is the player who, after five years, thinks he knows it all and lets up for a moment, who finds himself in appalling trouble.

Playing as one of an ensemble, whether it be of 8 or of 80, needs a special approach. In the first place the player must forget about being a soloist, and must submerge all personal characteristics of tempo because of the need to play in strict time with the rest of the orchestra as the conductor's beat demands. If a player—however good and possessing all manner of certificates and diplomas in his instrument—is suddenly pitched into an orchestra without much more experience than has been gained from the academy or college orchestra, he will very likely be unhappy and uneasy. He will have to play quietly so as not to stick out like a ragged end from the rest of the sound, and his sight-reading will very likely be poor, compared with this ability elsewhere among the players. If the new player is a string player, it may not matter so much; but if he is a wind player, he will not be pulling his weight for a long time. One can tell instantly when a player is unused to orchestral work, and in fact deputies are always booked with care and from among musicians who are 'known'. It is only when the orchestra is abroad, or there are epidemics or a sudden accident when the orchestra is in some remote place, that an unskilled player's efforts will lead to a real upset, because he will not have been booked with all the care of a normal occasion.

2
STRINGS

VIOLINS

THE FIRST VIOLINS SIT IN PAIRS ON THE CONDUCTOR'S left, extending from just under his left arm to sometimes the extreme left-hand corner of the platform. Needless to say, the more widely spaced they are, the more difficult it will be for those at the back to keep together with their senior colleagues at the front, where the decisions are taken. Each player is one of a pair, called a *desk*, but if there is an odd one—always at the back—he is called a *half-desk*. The senior member of each pair sits on the 'outside', that is to say on the audience side, and in the case of the first violins this is the right-hand person. The man who is at the front desk and on the outside is the *leader*, or in German countries, the *concert master* (*Konzertmeister*). He has a very taxing and responsible job, for not only has he to play his violin, he has to lead his section, to be followed by the second violins too, and to act as intermediary between the orchestra and the conductor. It is the leader who takes charge when the conductor is delayed, and may even be required to take the rehearsal himself; he is thanked by the conductor at the end of the concert, as representing the whole orchestra; he comes on alone to receive applause when the rest of the orchestra are settled; he decides when to get up to acknowledge applause, or when to leave the platform at the end—and until that time the orchestra must remain where they are. In unfortunate circumstances it is also the leader upon whom the orchestra rely when the conductor's directions are either ambiguous or incomprehensible. The leader is thus extremely important to everybody in the orchestra and to the conductor as well, and must never be found wanting. He may also be required to play solos where they occur in the score: not necessarily as in a violin concerto (although some leaders do so) but as, for instance, in Brahms's *First Symphony* or in Strauss's *Ein Heldenleben* (a fearsome part) or in

31

Delius's *First Dance Rhapsody*. In all these cases there is a new
line for solo violin above the normal first violin line in the score.
But overriding all these attributes which are expected of the
leader, it is his personality which comes to be reflected in the
orchestra as a whole.

There was once a celebrated leader of a great symphony
orchestra who ruled the musicians very strictly. His word was
law, and there was one invariable indication that his temper was
so frayed that it was about to give out. Just before the inevitable
explosion, usually caused by what he considered to be unnecessary over-rehearsal of a well-known work (Beethoven's *Seventh
Symphony* for example), this leader tipped back his chair and
rocked on the rear legs. Then he took the tiny end of a cigarette
from his mouth and flicked it with the point of his bow, and with
unerring accuracy, at the principal cello. This mild little man
had no cause to be the target, but the cigarette end always
finished up with him. At this, the leader announced that he
would rehearse the piece no more and prepared to leave. He
very nearly always won, too.

The leader's every-day companion at the front desk is the
sub-leader (at one time called the *Repetiteur*). Nowadays it can
even arise that there are two leaders or co-leaders, who never,
of course, play at the same concert, but share the very exhausting
role between them. In the event of the leader's absence, the sub-
leader takes his place. When they are there together and there
are markings to be done to their part (which they share on the
music stand between them), the sub-leader uses his pencil and
india-rubber, though the leader has a pencil handy too, so that
he can indicate special points which he may wish to remember
that concern him alone. Similarly, it is the inside player at each
desk who marks the part and turns the page for his colleague
at the outside of the desk, throughout the section. The markings
which they may have to make concern dynamics, whether
louder or softer; phrasing; speeding up and slowing down;
bowing marks and whether repeats at the end of movements are
to be played or not.

At the desk behind the leader and sub-leader—the second
desk—sit No 3 and No 4. No 3 is a sub-principal and is invariably paid a special salary to cover the eventuality of his having
to go up and sit at the exposed front desk. This is called *stepping-*

up. In symphony orchestras, positions are often specially 'paid' back to No 6 in the first violins, each player at the first three desks having a different salary. From there and backwards to the last desk is known as the *Rank and File*, a military-sounding title which is none the less accurate because a good string section performs exactly like a well-drilled squad of soldiers, and both are a joy to behold.

Playing stringed instruments has been described as 'drawing the sounds of a cat through its guts with the tail of a horse'—an unkind way of saying that a violin bow is made of horsehair and that the violin strings were once all made of gut (cow-gut, not catgut). Nowadays the lower strings are wire-spun nylon, but the top (or E) string is all wire. The resultant loss of richness is mourned by mainly non-string players, since the man-made fibres are far more reliable and tend not to break in the middle of a concert as gut strings had a habit of doing. It used to be eye-catching to watch a soloist, who had lost a string, snatch the leader's instrument and hand his own over, and to watch the priceless violin being handed back from one desk to the next, to be carried away to a place of safety, while another fiddle was ferried up to replace the one taken from the front desk. The total force of a strung and tuned violin is about 60 lb of tension.

The word 'fiddle' is in common parlance among violinists, and it also applies to the viola. Coming from a non-fiddle-player, though, it may not always be taken to kindly (as you may remember in that delightful children's musical tale 'Tubby the Tuba'). It originates in the Latin word 'fides' (a string) and its diminutive 'fidicula', which in turn gave way to the mediaeval 'fidel', hence 'fiddle'. Concurrently with this, in southern Europe, 'fidicula' gave way to 'fidula' and then 'viola', 'violin' and 'violoncello'.

The violinist in the photo facing page 48 is sitting in the conventional position and is playing the violin: a common enough sight. Look closely at the instrument, and see how beautifully it is designed to make the whole violin a succession of smoothly curved lines, with only the base of the bridge and the pegs registering as straight. A violinist will generally turn an instrument over when examining it, to look at the grain of the wood on its back, and also to scrutinise the varnish. Yet it is not the most beautiful instrument which yields the finest sound:

as Leopold Mozart said, 'To choose a fiddle for its outward symmetry and varnish is like choosing a singing bird for its fine feathers'. The science of violin sound and of the classical violin makers is a book in itself.

The violin is played by being tucked under the instrumentalist's chin, and the bow passed (with the right hand) across the strings. Minute hooks on each of the horsehairs set the strings vibrating. The sound is magnified by the hollow body of the violin and comes out of the two holes (shaped like the letter 'f'), one on each side of the 'table' and flanking the bridge. The left hand holds the 'neck' with the thumb on one side, which is not otherwise used, and the four fingers press down on the four strings to select the required note or notes.

Because the violin is the smallest of the stringed instruments, and is able to reach the highest notes without the use of *harmonics* (and many higher ones still by this method), it appears to be the most delicate in total visual effect when compared with its larger relatives, the viola, cello and double bass.

There are seventy different single elements which go to make up a violin, and these may be found enumerated in any book on

Cost of making a 'cheaper' violin
M. Thibouville-Lamy of Mirecourt, Paris and London
(the principal fiddle maker of our time)

	s	d
Wood for back		2
Wood for belly		2
Wood for neck		1
Workmanship in neck		2
Blackened fingerboard		2
Workmanship of back and belly		3
Cutting out by saw		1½
Shaping back and belly by machinery	1	0
Varnish		10
Fitting up, strings, bridge and tail-piece		9½
	3	9
6% for general expenses		3
	4	0
15% profit		8
	4	8

the instrument. The first edition of *Grove's Dictionary of Music and Muscians* (1889) gives a list of them, as well as the very amusing invoice on page 34.

The long article goes on 'Ludicrously low as this estimate is, it is certain that one of these fiddles, if carefully set up, can be made to discourse very tolerable music'. It should be observed that today (1974), the cheapest violins that can be bought in London from Messrs Boosey & Hawkes, cost £10.50 (made in China) or £25 (made in Germany).

New fiddles are not cheap, even when they are those sickly, mass-produced objects seen in shop windows alongside guitars and drum-kits. They never look well beside seasoned veterans of hundreds of concerts. In any case they cannot be described in the same way, in that a good violin has a proper name, the name of its maker. I was once with a violinist in a musicians' pub in London. He was accompanied by his instrument in its case. A stranger walked in, an odd-looking sort of man, carrying a vivid orange-painted fiddle-case, all done over in gloss. My companion and I gasped. He came up to us, and the conversation went something like this: He said: 'Mornin'!'

We said: 'What have you got in there, then?' (Introductory, interested question from one violinist to another.)

'Same as you, I expect,' the man replied, pointing to my companion's case, though most suspiciously, as if he were implying that he was out of an American gangster film.

'What is it then?' I asked.

'Bleedin' violin, of course,' he said, and turned his back on us.

At our laughter, he looked most threatening and walked out, taking with him the weirdest fiddle-case either of us had ever seen. He was an amateur, and either had no instrument there at all, or else did not care to reveal its impoverished appearance. But I shall never forget the sight of that case.

A few musicians make their own fiddles, and because they are executants, the results can be excellent. But even if they sell them after two years or so on the work-bench, it does nothing to stem the demand. It is a question of cash, and many a player now reduced to an inferior position in a section would probably be able to advance himself with a better instrument. An inferior one is sometimes referred to as 'that old box he's playing'.

As with stringed instruments, there is also a shortage of

really good string players. However, an enterprising teacher (of violins especially) in Japan called Mr Suzuki, is turning out hundreds of technically well-equipped players who have been learning from the moment they were able to walk, as part of life, like talking. Soon they are certain to invade Europe, and will be found to be much more highly accomplished than products of, for example, the old-fashioned Royal College of Music and Royal Academy of Music.

The second violins play the second voice in the four-part harmony, which relegates them to a subordinate place behind the firsts. Unfortunately, 'to play second fiddle' is a common expression used to describe someone or something inferior. The second violins in an orchestra are not this, although they generally have a less interesting time by filling in the harmonies and the rhythmic texture. If the violins are playing in waltz time, the first violins play the melody, with special emphasis on the 1st beat of the bar, while the seconds play only on the 2nd and 3rd beats. Hence their own description of their work as 'cha, cha'. The principal second violin is seated so that he can watch the leader, who is almost of greater importance to him than the conductor, for the leader is responsible for all the violins, not only his own section. The principal second is a highly skilled player, who may have been promoted from about No 4 or No 5 position in the firsts. The sub-principal second, possibly one of the most thankless sub-principal jobs in the whole orchestra, must be prepared to step-up to principal second as and when required. The rest of the section, always slightly smaller in number than the firsts, have no special features, save that the players at the back desks tend to be the very oldest or the very youngest members of the two violin sections. Without a doubt, the violin sections are the hardest worked in the orchestra in that they are seldom silent, or *tacet*. One very unusual example is in Fauré's *Requiem*, when they have a very long rest at the start of the work. When they eventually come in, the two violin sections play as one and the instrumentation of the work is:

2.0.2.2., 4.2.3., timps. 2 hp. org. Str.

(if you can work that out!)

VIOLAS

The next string section is a group once called the cinderellas of
the orchestra, the violas. They are not so neglected now in
specialist compositions, nor in major twentieth-century compositions either, thanks largely to the efforts of Paul Hindemith
(himself a violist) and of Lionel Tertis. They both showed the
world that the viola is not only a most important instrument
but also a very beautiful one when in the right hands, and when
playing music written knowingly for it. Of all instruments in the
orchestra, the viola is the only one which carries the name of a
flower. In size it is larger than the violin, and its sound is
richer and darker, though less bright because its size is not in
proportion to its deeper pitch. Were it so, the instrument
would have to be more like a small cello, and thus could not
possibly be held under the chin. In any event, because it is
larger than even the largest violin in breadth and in length (and
violins do vary in size), the violist's left arm has to be held out
further and has a greater weight to support than a violinist's.
Consequently it does not follow that a player accustomed to the
violin can pick up a viola and achieve the same success. Although such an eminent violinist as Yehudi Menuhin has
played viola concertos, he sounds much happier with the smaller
instrument.

There was once an occasion when a London orchestra was
going to record Brahms's *Second Serenade*. This work has no
violins; the top string line is taken by the violas throughout.
It was going to be necessary for this orchestra's viola section to
be augmented, and a person from the recording company
insisted that the best way to do this was to employ the un-
wanted violinists from the orchestra, equipped with violas.
Nothing could have been more absurd. The violinists did not
possess violas, they were not accustomed to playing violas, they
did not wish to play violas, nor did the violists want any such
usurpers in their section. So the requisite number of violists was
obtained from the freelance market, and the section was made up
of fine and experienced viola players.

It is not often that the violas can be identified when they are
playing in an orchestral composition because, as it has been said,
their sound is not bright, and it is only when they are given

something exposed to play that they can be picked out. Because their most valuable area of sound lies below that of the violins, viola parts are written in the alto clef with the treble clef employed only at the top of their range.

The foregoing may read in a slightly disparaging way to the violas, as if they are not really necessary in the orchestra. Of

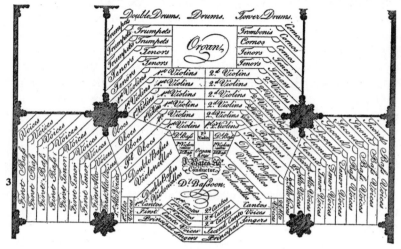

Fig. 4. Drawing which shows an orchestral layout of 1784

course they are. First and foremost the viola is the third or tenor voice in the string quartet, the four-part harmony of the string section that is so important to give a true and complete chord that is in turn repeated through the wind and brass sections and demonstrated by the four horns. In the eighteenth century the violas were known as the 'tenors', and we see them so named in Fig. 4, above. Without the violas, the two sections of violins and the cellos would be a 'voice' short, and that would never do. The viola is tuned C, G, D and A, as opposed to the violin's tuning of G, D, A and E.

CELLOS

While the violas have not the capacity to 'shine', the cello is quite large enough to be a true solo instrument. Of all the

stringed instruments it is the one which sounds by far the
foullest when badly played, while in the hands of a master, it
can be divine. As you can see from the photo facing page 48,
the cellist plays his instrument sitting down. If you watch him
take his seat, he will look down on the floor and move his cello
about as if prodding round for something. He is choosing the
best spot in which to put the spike that is fixed to the bottom of
the cello and hold it in place as a 'third leg' while it is being
played. This is unless the player is accustomed to the old-
fashioned cello-board, a flat piece of wood with a hole at each
end, into one of which the cello-spike fits, the other secured by
being put round one leg of the chair on which the player is
sitting. If, however, he is not using a cello-board, the musician
can still manage provided that he has chosen the spot for his
spike with care. If not, or if he moves about too much while
playing, thereby putting too much weight on the cello, it can
come adrift from its temporary hole in the floor and shoot forward, causing him to fall off his chair. Such an incident is very
comical to see, but it can do damage to the player and, more
important still, to his instrument. The spike, or tail-pin as it is
more properly called, only came into fashion in the 1890s.
Before then the cellist always held his instrument off the floor,
grasping it between his knees like a good horseman.

Cello music is generally written in the bass clef, but sometimes the tenor clef is found, and also the alto clef for the top of
the instrument's compass. The player is even asked to play in
the G or treble clef as well. Although the cello lies closer in
range to the viola than to the violin, it makes an excellent
partner to the higher instrument. This is apparent from trios for
violin, cello and piano, but also orchestrally in double concertos, such as those by Brahms and Delius; and in addition
there is the *Triple Concerto* by Beethoven in which the violin-
cello-piano trio element is used as a solo team, together, in
pairs, or singly in concerto form.

Cello players tend to be good-natured people, full of fun and
possessing a real sense of humour. While it may sound odd to
generalise like this, the playing of an instrument seems to lead
to a special kind of personality, or sub-personality in each
player. But one 'cellist story' must be told: shortly after the
last war, when music was getting back into its stride again,

gramophone recordings were in full swing, due to the increased demand from a music-starved population and a new generation of music-conscious people. Records were still of the 78 kind, a slow business. On a certain day in the Kingsway Hall in London (still used for this purpose because of its fine acoustics) a female cellist was playing a concerto with a first-rate orchestra. She was understandably nervous and was taking it all very seriously. In between 'takes' that lasted between $3\frac{1}{2}$ and $4\frac{1}{2}$ minutes for each side of the record, the master 'wax' had to be carefully lifted off and a new blank placed on the recording turntable for the next section of the work to be engraved into it. Between one of these breaks, one of the rank and file cellists in the orchestra started to exhibit signs of great distress. At last he got to his feet, with his cello in his hand, and walked towards one of the two flights of steps which lead up from the body of the hall to the platform, upon which the soloist was placed. At the foot of the stairs there are carved, wooden posts and, with everybody's eyes upon him, the cellist lifted his instrument above his head and smashed it down upon one of the banister posts, reducing it to a tangle of unrecognisable fragments of wood and strings. Most of the orchestra were aghast, and thought he had gone mad, for no instrumentalist in his right mind would treat his instrument with anything but the profoundest respect and loving care. The poor soloist, already suffering from a certain amount of strain by the very nature of the recording itself, gave a shriek and promptly collapsed in hysterics. But it was all a joke—a black joke in the circumstances. The now shattered 'instrument' was a useless old cello, made up to look playable for this purpose. The session had to be abandoned until another day, when the practical joker was not in evidence.

There was once an instrument called the *Arpeggione*, something like a guitar with six strings, but played with a bow like a cello. It was invented in Vienna in 1823 by G. Staufer, and its strings were tuned in fourths from the E below the bass stave to the E above it. A year later, Schubert wrote a most delightful sonata for arpeggione and piano which is considered to be a typical example of his art. Had it not survived, it is doubtful whether the instrument would ever have been remembered because it never became accepted. The *Arpeggione Sonata in A* (Deutsch 821), is now played either on a cello or, more often still, on the viola, especially at auditions. Despite the fact that the arpeggione was played like a cello, violists claim that it lies better for them, an assertion which cellists dispute.

DOUBLE BASSES

Lastly, in the string department, we come to the monsters of the genre, the double basses, although nowadays these instruments are not as large as they once were. Their role is to reinforce the bass line played. Their part is written in the bass clef, but an octave higher than it sounds so as to avoid too many leger lines. Basses today have either four or five strings, the latter allowing for a greater flexibility in playing, for the same note can quite often be reached on more than two strings. An alternative to the 5-string bass is the 4-string bass 'with extension'. This is a mechanical contrivance which allows for the fourth string to be tuned down to a lower note by flipping over a catch at the top or peg end of the instrument. In fact the string is always tuned to that note, usually B or C, but the extension acts as a stop on the string, which then reverts to the normal, low E.

The distance between notes is greatly increased on this instrument, even when compared with the cello; but by comparison with the violin, when one is talking in terms of finger shifts of one sixteenth of an inch, the double bass involves shifts of a couple of inches. Precise accuracy of note-finding, or intonation, has thus to be sought no less carefully, but in a different fashion on the bass, whose area of search is greater and makes it far easier for the player to 'get away with' sloppy intonation.

There is also the register of the instrument to be considered. Its growling sound does not register as readily with the average ear, which is more accustomed to sounds in the region of middle C and above. There are relatively few solos for the double bass, partly because it is not all that pleasant to listen to on its own except when a really excellent player can bring its dark sound to life. An example of a solo is 'Elephants' in Saint-Saëns' *Carnival of Animals*. A young American bass player called Gary Karr plays a double bass concerto by Hans Werne Henze and he has also recorded and played in London a very amusing set of variations on themes from Rossini's *Mosè*. This is all virtuoso stuff for an instrument not normally considered for virtuoso work. Players as competent as Karr are very few and far between.

The father of the double bass was an Italian called Domenico Dragonetti, who still gives his name to a special way of holding the bow (photo facing p. 48), after the days when it was concave in shape. The picture on the right of this one shows the same man playing *pizzicato,* that is to say, plucking the string with the first finger of his left hand and thereby producing an altogether different sound from when the note is bowed. The abbreviation *pizz* in a part means that the note, phrase or section is to be played in this manner, and when normal bowing is to be resumed, it will then say *arco* or *coll'arco* (with bow). If there is no instruction, 'with bow' is implied. One of the best examples of full string strength pizzicato is in the third movement of Tchaikovsky's *Fourth Symphony.*

Really good stringed instruments are exceedingly hard to find today, and then they are only within the reach of players with either another good instrument to sell, or else a little capital to put down as deposit, and the necessary background to obtain a loan for the balance. Players are sentimental about their instruments, often preferring to pass them over to others who they know or admire, even if this is for less than could be obtained on the open market. There is indeed merit in this. Italy and Germany of the occupation were the last good sources to find instruments, but since then it has meant watching auction catalogues and obituary notices. The word gets round quickly in any case. And it is not only good instruments that players are after, but good bows too. String-players have the dealer's facility for remembering who owned certain important instruments, and their pedigrees for several generations. They know what these instruments sounded like and are always interested to follow their progress, especially when they have been overhauled.

Since only the largest orchestra can boast a double bass section of more than six regular players, we should mention here the question of rotation in the upper strings and cellos. 'Rotation' means the moving round of players to desks and positions where they are not accustomed to sitting, and also with a different partner. Generally, the idea of this is to give young or new players the opportunity of being heard by the senior members of the section. Thus if a first violinist is about to leave, the vacancy so caused might well be filled by a player already in the first or second violin section. So he is brought up to sit behind the leader or the principal second so that a better assessment of his worth can be made.

Regular rotation of players so that they can sit in every seat behind the first desk and round again until they are back where they started does wake up the people who are content to remain far back and untroubled by the excitement which is engendered near the front. Before long they find themselves up there too. And if the merit of any player is in doubt, he can be heard completely. This very rarely happens in the independent orchestras because they have fairly free hands to give their players notice if they want to; but in other orchestras it does prevent players at the back from becoming atrophied.

Sometimes a player will not wish to come forward in the section because he knows he owns an inferior instrument. Perhaps he cannot afford, or is too mean to buy a better one; but playing on a poor fiddle, or whatever it is, does impair the player's chances of promotion.

3
WOODWIND

THAT PART OF THE ORCHESTRA WHICH EXCLUDES THE strings and the percussion is called the wind, a term that embraces both woodwind and brass. Apart from the fact that some woodwind instruments are no longer made of wood and that brass instruments can look like silver ones, the situation is not changed at all. The purpose of this large and forceful body is to give a different colour to the overall sound. You may say that colour cannot be heard and does not apply to anything auditory, but it is nevertheless the best term we have to describe different sound 'personalities'. Where it is used visually to explain differences in light and shade and pigment, one can say that a pillar box looks 'bright' red or a pile of clay against a white wall looks 'harsh'. Similarly sounds can be described as 'bright' and 'harsh' and a good many other things as well. Even excluding this method of musical, descriptive colouring, the kinds of sounds which are made respectively by stringed, woodwind, brass and percussion instruments are all so different as to be obvious to any but the deaf. They have been developed over the centuries so as to enable composers to achieve the greatest variety of special sounds and 'tone colouring' available to them from the modern orchestra. In the case of woodwind instruments, which are our immediate concern, each instrument possesses different sound qualities at the top and at the bottom of its compass, almost like entirely different instruments.

Among the strings there is the quartet as a basic group to produce four-part harmony (often referred to in scores as 'string quartet' when it means first and second violins, violas and cellos) *en masse*; in the case of the woodwind the quartet is:

Flutes
Oboes
Clarinets
Bassoons

44

This already begins to sound like a musical version of *Happy Families*, and I recall reading something of the sort a long time ago. Now that I turn it up (from Bacharach's *A Musical Companion*) it reads very coyly, considering that W. R. Anderson wrote it as long ago as 1933–1934:

Family life is the essence of the orchestra's existence, and one has to remember that, when writing for it, making each group's harmony complete, as a rule. A beautiful example to mankind is the orchestra—families living in peace and personal dignity, self-contained and working together for good.

Oh, Mr Anderson, was it ever really like that?

Woodwind instruments have been developed over the years far more than any others. So that merely to say 'flute' or 'oboe' means the instruments known by those names today.

A wind player and especially a woodwind player expects to be called upon to play a second instrument in his section (flute to piccolo; oboe to cor anglais; clarinet to bass clarinet or clarinet to E♭ clarinet) and this is known as doubling. Doubling is paid for either within the player's contract (if he has one) or else per session, but not for the rehearsal. Doubling does not apply to the senior, or principal player in each section, who keeps to his one instrument all the time.

FLUTES

If you turn to the reproduction of a page of full-score on p. 25 you will see that the top line is occupied by *kl.Fl.* meaning 'little flute', better known outside Germany as the piccolo. 'Piccolo' is an Italian word meaning 'little', so there we are: *kleine* in German, and piccolo in Italian, qualifying the size of flute that is needed. Perhaps you know Gerard Hoffnung's marvellous cartoons of musical instruments and of people and instruments taking each others' identities. In the Artists' Bar at the Royal Festival Hall in London there are several large reproductions of Hoffnung's immensely witty and knowledgeable drawings on two of the walls, where they are set off into the infinite by having two looking glasses facing each other and at right-angles to the Hoffnungs. One of them shows a large, fat flautist carrying in his waistcoat pocket a tiny little man playing the piccolo.

All musical instruments 'speak' because either a mass or a column of air is set in motion by means of one kind of friction or another. In the case of the woodwind instruments, it is a column of air which is contained inside them and is normally either open or stopped. Flutes are open, and are blown into by the player across an aperture, while the instrument is held sideways above his right shoulder, nearly parallel with the floor. This blowing causes the air inside the tube to vibrate, and according to the length of the tube which is open to it, so the pitch of the note varies: the longer the column of air, the deeper the note, and vice versa. The length of the vibrating air column can be controlled by covering holes along the side of the instrument, in the same way as string players vary the length of the vibrating strings with their fingers. The lowest octave of the flute is not very strong and is rather 'thick' in sound. The second octave, which is obtained by 'overblowing' or blowing more strongly and at the same time modifying the fingering so as to produce an identical scale, but an octave higher, is far more strong and smooth, and is the best part of the flute's register. The third octave, obtained by a complicated technique known as 'cross-fingering', is very bright and penetrating. Certain aspects of the flute's behaviour are very convenient, like, for instance the fact that it goes into its next register (or 'overblows' to give this the right term) at the octave, and not anywhere else. As we shall discover, other wind instruments are not as accommodating. Also the flute is not a *transposing* instrument, that is to say its part is written in the exact key, and in the treble stave, in which it is required to play (see p. 53).

The piccolo, by virtue of its smaller size, can play higher notes than the flute, and can cut right through the orchestral sound and be heard skirling away at the top, adding great brightness to the total effect. Unlike the double bass, the piccolo's part is written an octave lower than it sounds, but for the same reason, which is to avoid too many leger lines—above the stave this time.

The concert flute was always made of wood and is one of the oldest forms of musical instruments still in use today. Its sound expresses simplicity, beauty and chastity, and its solo in Gluck's opera *Orpheus and Eurydice,* called 'The Dance of the Blessèd Spirits' is a good example of all these attributes. Today the instrument is not made of wood, but of a silver alloy, even of solid silver, which allows it to produce a cleaner and more brilliant sound than before. In addition, since the 1830s, the system of fingering has been improved by the use of a system devised by a Munich flautist called Theobald Boehm. The Boehm system is in general use by flautists and oboists, and even in some cases by clarinettists and bassoonists as well. It allows, by means of levers (called 'keys') with soft pads on the end, for holes that would not otherwise be within easy reach of the fingers, to be manipulated at speed, for their positioning must always be in the correct acoustic places along the instrument.

The flute is the simplest woodwind instrument in construction and is descended from the flûte à bec, which was held downwards and not crosswise, but whose sound was too frail to maintain its position in the orchestra. It is still in existence, however, as the recorder, a good instrument on which to learn the basic requirements of blowing, controlling air in the tube, and developing pure note-sounds. While recorders come in enough sizes to form recorder consorts (to my ear a dreadfully dreary occupation), the modern flute comes in three sizes: the concert flute, the piccolo and the alto flute.

In some languages, including English, the alto flute is known as the 'bass flute' since it corresponds to the concert flute in roughly the same manner as the viola does to the violin. Both flutes have the same relative compass, but the alto flute is pitched a fourth lower, and for this reason it is a transposing instrument (see p. 53). It looks much larger than the normal flute and instead of being straight, it has a curved extension on the end further from the aperture. It also has a very dark and hollow sound, and is not very often seen.

OBOES

While the flute occupies the top line in the four-part harmony of the woodwind section, the second line is taken by the oboe. Now we have a different conception of four-part harmony, for each principal woodwind player is a soloist in his own right, but on occasions has to fulfil the duty of making up the quartet of sound. It must also be added that the tonal quality of these instruments differ greatly from one another, whereas in the case of the first two voices in the string quartet, they are the same type of instrument entirely, namely violins.

The unusual name of oboe derives from the French word *hautbois*, although precursors of that instrument are known to have existed at least as early as Roman times. Ancient descriptions have claimed that it was extremely strident, and could compete with the trumpet for penetrative quality. An oboe can still cut through the orchestral texture, but with more grace and delicacy, even femininity, than hitherto, if the accomplishments of the Roman hautbois are to be believed.

While the flutes are 'open' instruments, in which the sound vibrates more or less naturally in the tube or 'flue-pipe', the oboe is constructed on the principle of a conical tube down which the air is blown through a double reed. The mouthpiece of the oboe, in which the reed is set, is very thin, so that a good deal of air pressure is required to keep up a constant supply through the reed and into the tube of the instrument. This is why you often see oboe players with their cheeks puffed out like frogs: they have to conserve a reservoir of air inside their mouths all the time, so that they are never in danger of running short. This all takes a time to acquire, and to be able to rely on as a technique. While the oboe is being played, it is held downwards at an angle of about 20 degrees from the horizontal, but you may occasionally see the instrument's bell pointing at you when the player seeks to achieve greater volume or emphasis of sound.

Fingering is more or less the same for the oboe as it is for the flute, though of course one instrument is played vertically and the other horizontally, roughly speaking. The oboe has a richer, stronger, more vibrant quality too, and of course it is the oboe which gives the tuning note (the A above middle C) for the whole orchestra (unless there is a keyboard instrument there). The next time you hear Beethoven's *Seventh Symphony*, notice the oboe's characteristic start to the whole work.

The oboe is not a transposing instrument and, like the flute, has its natural or 'home' key in D. The question of its subtlety of sound depends upon the kind of reed used. This is a sliver of cane, and both its quality and thickness can affect the whole

(above) *The string quartet, showing from left to right, 1st and 2nd violins, viola and cello;* (below) *the bass, showing from left to right, normal hold,* **D***ragonetti hold and pizzicato*

Woodwind: (above), *from l[eft]* *to right, flute, oboe, clari[net]* (*Eb and Bb*), *bassoon;* (left[)] *bassoon and contra bassoon[.]*

colouring of the instrument. German oboists, like the virtuoso Hans Holliger, prefer a wide reed, and get a correspondingly 'thicker' sound; while the French opt for a narrower one with its correspondingly more delicate speech. We shall discover later, when dealing with the clarinets, that they have the same problems over reeds, but not the same kind of reeds at all.

The making of reeds is the individual player's own responsibility and three out of the four sections of woodwind players have the constant thought in their minds that their reed may not survive the work they are playing. It is a constant nag which can be diminished only as a player becomes more experienced, although there is such a thing as a reed-machine nowadays. Even so, unfriendly temperatures or humidity in the studio or concert hall can play havoc with the best of reeds.

There was once an oboe player who returned home to his parents after a gap of a couple of years, long enough for them to have forgotten what it was like to have him living there. He spent the whole of one morning in his 'old room', making reeds, and was very pleased with the result. He went out for a breath of fresh air, leaving everything as it was, but on his return his mother told him that at last she had been able to get into his 'old room', and had tidied up and thrown away 'all those little bits of wood'. Busy little woman!

Before a rehearsal or a concert, you will see an oboist with the reed (inside the mouthpiece) in his mouth already, warming it up and 'getting it going'. Brass players do the same with their mouthpieces. So it is evident that orchestral musicians do not merely get their instruments out of their cases, play them, and put them back again until next time. There is always a great deal of care and attention needed to enable the instruments to sound at their best so that their owners can rely on their behaving properly for a whole session.

The oboe's big brother in terms of size and depth of tone is the cor anglais, which is neither English, nor a horn. It is a reminder of the old 'chalumeau' of Gluck's day, now entirely disappeared. The 'cor', as musicians call it, has a particularly mournful, but rich and fairly fruity tone, in the nicest sense of the word. It is, to all intents and purposes, an alto oboe. You will recognise it as the solo instrument in Sibelius's *Swan of Tuonela* and in the Overture to Rossini's *William Tell*. On account of its

size, the cor's length is adjusted to the player's comfort by having
its mouthpiece bent backwards towards his mouth. This is at the
end of a steel tube that encloses the reed. Otherwise its fingering
is the same as that of the oboe, though its compass is a fifth
lower, making it a transposing instrument (see page 53) and
calling for its music to be written a fifth higher than it 'sounds'.
Nor is its bell-end the same as an oboe's at all. The lower end of
the cor swells out into a pear shape and ends with a far more
constricted opening, so helping to give it that particular sound
quality.

If there are two oboe players in an orchestra, the second one is
required sometimes to double on cor. If there are three or four
oboists, it is the last one who plays cor. Cor players quite often
see themselves as nearly failed first oboists and their only wish
is to set the cor aside and concentrate on the one instrument. Yet
apart from this, a good cor player has a most gratifying time
with several very rewarding solos in the repertory, but with the
need to have and to maintain two instruments.

If you read down a full score, you will see that the clarinets
follow the oboes, who in turn follow the flutes. But I am going
to leave the clarinets last, for several reasons, and go from the
oboes to the bassoons, especially as they are of the same construction and require something approximating the same technique in blowing.

BASSOONS

The bassoon is the lower or bass member of the woodwind
quartet, lower in compass than the cello, its counterpart in the
string quartet. Were the tube of the bassoon to be straightened
out, it would be unmanageable for one person in its eight feet of
polished wood. So it is bent back upon itself to a little over four
feet, and yet still requires a strap to go round the player's neck
for support, and leaving a foot-long silver mouthpiece ending
in the double reed. The bell of the instrument is up in the air
and its 'butt' down below the player's right thigh, a few inches
above the floor. The bassoon is known in both German and
Italian as 'Faggot' because of its resemblance to a bundle of
sticks. This comic implication goes further in the tone of the

instrument at the top of its register, where it emulates the braying of Bottom and the antics of the comedians in Mendelssohn's music for *A Midsummer Night's Dream*; the multiplication of the broomsticks in Dukas's *L'Apprenti Sorcier*; and in the harrowing goings-on during Malcolm Arnold's Overture *Tam O'Shanter*, where it signifies the drunken Tam. On the other hand the bassoon is able to sound most plaintive, as in its opening solo to the aria 'Una furtiva lagrima' from Donizetti's opera *L'Elisir d'Amore*. A last example of it in parodying mood, is as the old and obviously impotent grandfather in Prokofiev's *Peter and the Wolf*. But in concertos by Mozart and Weber, the instrument comes into its own with great surety.

The bassoon, however, is a most capricious instrument to play in tune, for the science of acoustics does not apply as strongly as elsewhere, even allowing for the fact that it is a rogue science at the best of times. Furthermore, every good bassoon is constructed slightly differently from any other, thus making it a unique combination of player and instrument. At certain moments in its wide range of over $3\frac{1}{2}$ octaves, the bassoon can offer the player the alternative of obtaining a single note in several different ways, and the player must judge which method is best suited to the particular tonal quality or agility required at that moment. Although it looks a cumbersome instrument, the bassoon can really allow of great speed of execution, but it is not easy to learn and to become proficient in. The player needs an exceptionally good ear too, so as to be able to adjust his intonation to the bassoon's own waywardness. It is not a transposing instrument, being notated in the bass clef with occasional use of the tenor (or F) clef for its upper register.

Even so, it is not the deepest of the wind instruments, for its much larger, much more faggotty-looking relative, the contrabassoon, can go down to the B♭, an octave and a fifth below the bass stave. Bassoonists just call it the 'contra' although you may see it referred to as the 'double-bassoon' since it goes down an octave lower than the ordinary bassoon. It measures sixteen feet four inches long, but is folded back on itself four times to produce an instrument of about the same practical length as the bassoon. The fingering is roughly the same, and generally one finds that a contra-player is equally at home on the higher instrument. Like the double bass, the contra speaks an octave lower than its

Fig. 5. Six bars from an orchestral score showing rationalised notation as in a Penguin score

music is written, and it is thus a simple transposing instrument by one octave. Beethoven made most effective use of it in the grave-digging scene in *Fidelio*, and to reinforce the solidity of woodwind in the last movements of the *Fifth* and *Ninth Symphonies*.

The larger the woodwind instrument, the more it is affected by cold weather. At Covent Garden Opera House in London after the last war, when power cuts were particularly common, the players used to have to rehearse in overcoats. While these garments seriously restricted the arm movements of string players, the freezing conditions prevented the bassoons from operating normally, so that they spoke a fraction late all the time. The conductor understood the reason well, and was sympathetic, but

Fig. 6. The same six bars (as left) notated normally

it was some time before these faggots were well enough warmed
to give off their usual sparks.

Transposing Instruments

A transposing instrument is one that plays a different note from
that actually written in the part. If we consider a B♭ clarinet,

for example, the printed note C would sound as B♭ on this instrument. The reason for this lies in the nature of the instrument and its construction. The best tone quality and ease of playing and blowing and over-blowing in this particular instrument necessitates its being 'based' on B♭. This is its home key and it has consequently to be adapted by the player, who transposes at sight, from practice and without any difficulty, to bring it up by one tone to the rest of the orchestra. But this is not all. A clarinet player has another instrument with its home key in A, that he uses according to the demands of the music and its key and accidentals, for the A clarinet, as it is called, has to be brought up by a minor third. There is an easy way to remember what to do about all this by the little rhyme:

'So much below C
So much above the key'

The acoustic reasons for transposition need not detain us here any further, except to demolish the theory that if an instrument is constructed in C it is bound to be all right. It isn't, and this is precisely why clarinets in C, which used to exist, have been abandoned because of their poor sound quality, and the A and B♭ transposing instruments reign supreme.

Although we have not yet dealt with all the instruments, it might be helpful to set out the names and pitches of the transposing instruments. Various efforts have been made to rationalise scores by printing all notes as they sound and ignoring the vagaries of those instruments under discussion. Penguin Books Ltd. was the last firm to attempt it, and a reproduction from one of its scores is shown in Fig. 5, p. 52. This may have been a great help to those unaccustomed to score-reading, but it merely makes a bugbear out of something which is not. I would rather suggest that if you are worried by it all, you practise reading a proper score, and you will find it is not nearly as cumbersome as you once thought, or as it might appear to start with. Fig. 6 on p. 53 shows the same excerpt as Fig 5, but notated normally.

Horn and clarinet players are probably the most proficient in the art of transposition, as indeed conductors themselves have to be. Many a young or a new conductor has been quizzed about a note in an effort to catch him out. He will invariably answer by asking another question: 'As printed or as sounding?' This may give him a moment longer in which to work out and check the answer, or else to make certain that he has been asked a fair question. It is, after all, scarcely different from mastering the alto and tenor clefs when you have been brought up solely on the treble and bass.

Piccolo	Written an octave lower than it sounds
Alto (bass) Flute	Written a fourth higher than it sounds
Cor anglais	Written a fifth higher than it sounds
Oboe d'Amore	Written a minor third higher than it sounds
Heckelphone	Written in the treble clef, an octave higher than it sounds
Sarrusophone in B♭	Written a tone higher than it sounds
Sarrusophone in E♭	Written a minor third lower than it sounds
Clarinet in B♭	Written a tone higher than it sounds
Clarinet in A	Written a minor third higher than it sounds
Clarinet in E♭	Written a minor third lower than it sounds
Bass Clarinet	Written a ninth higher than it sounds, in the treble clef
Basset Horn	Written in the treble clef a fifth higher than it sounds
Saxophone in B♭	Written a tone higher than it sounds
Saxophone in E♭	Written a minor third lower than it sounds
Horn in F	Written without key signature, in the treble clef, a perfect fifth higher than it sounds and with all accidentals notated
The Human Voice	is the perfect transposing instrument, for unless the singer possesses the most acute perfect pitch, he or she can sing at sight from any key to any key, once having been given a starting note.

CLARINETS

The name 'clarinet' means a 'little trumpet', which is not the case, although we have heard some players of the instrument doing their best to make it seem so. It is the last instrument to be accepted into the symphony orchestra, having first appeared in about 1690 in Nuremberg. It is also the first common instrument, reading down the score, which transposes.

We have heard that the flute 'overblows' at the octave, that is to say it goes into its next register, very conveniently, at this point. In order for a wind player to overblow, he alters his fingering and gives a different pressure with his lips, thus making the sound rise into the next octave, or else into the one above that. Anybody who has blown a recorder will be familiar with the procedure.

In the case of the clarinet, however, this overblowing does not happen at the octave, but at the octave and a fifth, since the instrument is constructed very differently from the flute. Between the low octave of its compass and until it does overblow, the clarinet is at its weakest so far as its tone is concerned, and the fingering is awkward too. But above this area lies the best part of the instrument's capabilities of another two octaves. Even so, some lovely dark notes are to be found in the clarinet's lowest register, which is known as its 'chalumeau' tone, after that antique instrument mentioned on page 49.

The clarinet's speed of execution, its gradations of crescendo and diminuendo, and the available volume or pianissimo of sound, make it altogether a most flexible and agile instrument. Remember the initial upwards *glissando* (or seamless slide) of the solo clarinet at the start of Gershwin's *Rhapsody in Blue*?

The clarinet has a single reed in a closed mouthpiece which 'stops' the tube and so gives it the lower register, which Prokofiev used to such good effect to illustrate the cat in *Peter and the Wolf*, 'creeping forward on her velvet paws'. In its middle register the clarinet is rich and smooth and creamy; at the upper end it is shrill and piercing.

Clarinets come in four main kinds. The A and B♭ are virtually interchangeable and form the basic instruments in the section. The B♭ instrument (or 'B' as it is called by players because B♭ is called B in Germany while B♮ is known as H) lessens the number of flats in a flat key by two, while the A instrument lessens the number of sharps by three. So a player will select the better instrument for his purpose, depending on the key signature of the work before him. There used to be a C clarinet, which of course did not need to transpose, but the fact that it was made to suit the key also made it clear that the key did not suit *it*, and it fell into disuse because it was a poor instrument by comparison with the other two.

The use of two instruments within a short space of time and often in one composition, means that both of them have to be kept warmed up. Cold weather and draughts affect the precision of pitch. Uses of the clarinet are legion, but Mozart was the first composer to show off its powers. His *Clarinet Concerto* and *Clarinet Quintet* are two special examples, while his *Symphony No 40 in G minor* was scored first without them, and then with. The former version is seldom heard.

In America particularly the 'B' instrument alone is used, due to the players' superior technique and efficiency, and this does save the awkwardness of two instruments being carried about and warmed up.

The other two clarinets most often met in the concert hall are the E♭ and the bass. The first is somewhat smaller than the 'B' or the A, and in consequence it has a shorter pipe and higher compass. It is pitched a perfect fourth above the 'B' instrument and of course is a transposing instrument as well. It is believed to have first been used in a symphonic work on 5 December 1830 when Berlioz incorporated it in his première of the *Symphonie Fantastique* in Paris. This was in the last movement, called the 'Witches' Sabbath'. It has a very incisive and shrill quality that illustrates both the comic and the sinister or tragic, both elements which it again underlines in Richard Strauss's *Till Eulenspiegel*. It originated as a military band instrument.

The largest clarinet in common use is the bass, which has a range that starts an octave below the 'B', or sometimes the A. It does not look like the other clarinets because the lower end of the tube is curved upwards and outwards to end in a bell. The upper end has a metal tube fixed on to it and it is bent down again and towards the player's mouth. Looked at from a distance you might be excused for thinking the bass clarinet is a kind of saxophone, and indeed there is a connection between these two instruments, as we shall see in a moment.

Music for the bass clarinet is written in the treble clef, a major ninth above the actual pitch. This clef may seem an odd way to notate a bass instrument, but at least it does conform with all the other clarinets. Some French scores still have it notated a different way, but that need not concern us because as a rule such parts are rewritten.

A kind of tenor clarinet, not often seen, is called the basset horn. Its name is derived from the fact that an instrument-maker called Horn produced his little bass—or 'basset'—clarinet in

1770 (the year in which Beethoven was born) and so the name stuck. It has a not very sensitive sound, but Mozart used it in his *Magic Flute* and his *Requiem*. In its Italian version of corno di bassetto, it became the pen name of George Bernard Shaw, music critic. The other members of the clarinet family need not concern us here because they are so rarely seen or heard, but all clarinets are associated with saxophones, as I have implied.

Although the saxophone is more generally thought of in terms of the dance-band than of the orchestra, it was intended by its inventor, a Belgian called Adolphe Sax, for serious use. Of all contexts, its first use seems to have been in a biblical oratorio called *The Last King of Judah* by the French composer J. G. Kastner in 1844.

The saxophone has nevertheless come back into its more serious or caricaturing use since it was snatched away for rag-time. Claude Debussy wrote a *Rhapsody for Saxophone and Orchestra* and so did Eric Coates. Strauss calls for a quartet of them in his *Symphonia domestica*. Vaughan Williams calls for a solo saxophone in his ballet *Job* to illustrate the insincere and wheedling voices of Job's comforters. All the same, there are few important symphonic works for the saxophone; one work, by Ernest Tomlinson, is for four solo saxes and orchestra, by no means easy to play, especially for the saxophones, which need virtuoso treatment. The main reason why the instrument is not used more is because its sound does not blend with others in the orchestra, and either obtrudes too much, or else has to be used in a solo capacity. This is awkward, and so it fails to be a representative member of the otherwise obliging instruments which allow themselves to be heard when required, and otherwise can be subdued comfortably among the rest. It is not surprising that the saxophone has unusual accomplishments because it is an utterly hybrid instrument. It has a single clarinet reed, the conical tube of the oboe family, clarinet fingering and a brass tube with out-thrown bell like a bass clarinet. Furthermore it transposes, whether it is the instrument in 'B' or in E♭. It strikes one as if it was designed by a committee—like a camel.

Clarinettists are invariably an extrovert lot. This is a generalisation, which I know is dangerous though I can think of only one exception, by way of defence. Two of the leading clarinet players of the time are Jack Brymer and Gervase de Peyer. Brymer had been with the BBC Symphony Orchestra for many years before becoming disenchanted with the 'new music', and seeking a more romantic turn to his musical life, with the LSO. Boulez checked Brymer for the way in which he was playing a phrase in one of his own compositions, and Brymer seemed unable to get it right. Boulez then sang him the phrase. Brymer took his clarinet from his mouth and said: 'Oh, you mean like this . . .?' and sang the phrase as well. 'Yes, that's right' replied Boulez.

'Well now that we can both sing it', said Brymer, 'you'd better find somebody who can play it.'

Gervase de Peyer is a different kind of person altogether. He was formerly principal clarinet of the LSO, before Brymer went there. He had a busy life with recitals, chamber music and conducting and used to tell the LSO when he was free, rather than giving them the first choice of his dates. Naturally they were rather annoyed and decided to engage a co-principal clarinet to lead the section when de Peyer was absent. The prospective new entrant, Bernard Walton, (now unfortunately no longer with us) was with the RPO, and the LSO attempted to entice him to them. The RPO wanted to keep Walton, and a bit of jacking up of salary went on at one end, with negotiations about numbers of concertos a year coming from the other. de Peyer was understandably alarmed when he heard about the concerto clause, because *he* wanted to play any clarinet concerto that was going with the LSO, and they do not bill one often. So in the end it all came to grief. Walton stayed with the RPO, and not long afterwards de Peyer left the LSO.

Before ending this chapter about the woodwind, it might be useful to spend a moment on several existing variants of the normal instruments still seen at concerts. There are no other flutes, but there are several other oboes. (Note that while the correct, grammatical plural of oboe is *oboi*, they are never called that, and it would be considered ridiculous to do so.)

Richard Strauss was probably the last great adventurer in orchestration since Wagner, and his use of instruments both old and new bears close study. In his *Symphonia domestica* he demands a total woodwind force of:

piccolo
2 flutes
2 oboes
oboe d'amore
cor anglais
clarinet in D
clarinets in B♭ and A
bass clarinet
4 saxophones (sop, alt, ten, bs.)
2 bassoons
contra bassoon

One of the reasons for these extravagant demands was that Strauss never stopped trying—and he generally succeeded completely—to imitate actual sounds in music.

Among the instruments above you will find the oboe d'amore, which is a rare instrument that Strauss lifted out of a silence that had existed round it since the time of Bach. It sounds a minor third lower than the oboe and is thus notated a minor third higher than it sounds, therefore becoming a transposing oboe. It has a hollow, globular bell instead of an open, conical one like the oboe, and it possesses a rather sad, veiled tonal quality.

Then there is the heckelphone, a baritone oboe which Delius requires in his *First Dance Rhapsody*, and in his *Requiem*. In both cases he refers to it as 'bass oboe', which it is not. Strauss asks for the heckelphone too, in *Salome*, in *Elektra* and in his ballet *Josephslegende* which uses a number of weird, quasi-antique wind instruments. The heckelphone's pitch lies between that of the cor anglais and the bassoon, and it is of German origin, named after its inventor Wilhelm Heckel. It has a body not only twice as long as an oboe, but also twice as wide. It ends in a closed, spherical-shaped bell which has to rest upon a stand. Its bassoon reed gives it a smooth tone that is, at the same time, more brilliant than that of the bassoon and more 'masculine' than the oboe, with which it can often be confused.

The true bass oboe is an entirely different instrument. It is French in origin and correspondingly fragile in construction, in reed and in sound, rather like a larger version of the cor anglais. While the heckelphone can make its presence felt in the orchestra, the bass oboe is not robust enough to do so, and its presence, from a purely listening aspect, is liable to be overlooked.

The sarrusophone (not to be confused with the sousaphone) is another cousin of the oboe, constructed in the same way, but made of brass. This hybrid comes in about six or eight sizes and was originally intended to give more body in military bands to supplement the otherwise wooden oboes. This idea came from a French bandmaster called Sarrus, who brought out his prototype sarrusophone in 1863. Because of their band origin, all sarrusophones are either in B♭ or E♭ and transpose accordingly, some by as much as two octaves.

It is unlikely that you will be fortunate enough to see and hear a sarrusophone on the concert platform, but it might just happen as it has done very occasionally in the past. Sir Thomas Beecham (to whom almost everything musical happened at one time or another in his long professional life) tells a wonderful story about an occasion when he needed the instrument for a work by Joseph Holbrooke called *Apollo and the Seaman*, and the difficulty he had in finding someone to play it. Holbrooke and Beecham set out together to Paris on their search where

enshrined in a tiny apartment and surrounded by, indeed almost buried beneath, dozens of weird-looking instruments was an equally diminutive old man of gentle and venerable appearance to whom we made known the reason for our visit. To our intense relief he accepted our offer of an engagement with alacrity, declaring that such an event would be a worthy climax to a long career spent in the service of the Republic, and going so far in his enthusiasm as to toy with the idea that Providence had chosen him out as an apostle to convey a special branch of Gallic culture to the less enlightened shores of Great Britain . . . On returning to England I began with ardour the task of realising in rehearsal and performance the artistic problem of *Apollo and the Seaman* . . . The band parts, which had been copied with reckless celerity, teemed with errors of every sort . . . In the midst of it all arrived the venerable sarrusophonist, who at once became an especial object of interest to the rest of the players and the recipient of an excess of hospitality which for a few days deprived us of his company. Meanwhile it had been discovered that he had brought over the wrong set of instruments (there seemed to be as many in the family as there are names in a Biblical genealogy), which further delayed his participation in the proceedings: and even when the right ones did arrive they were to my ears almost inaudible in the sea of sound that surged about me . . . On the whole this remarkable experiment went off satisfactorily . . . and the only accident of any consequence I noticed . . . was that which befell our aged friend from across the Channel. Excited and bewildered by his novel surroundings, he missed his first important lead and after several wild efforts to come in at the wrong place, which were promptly supressed by his adjoining colleagues, gave up despairingly and remained tacit for the rest of the evening . . . He returned to his native land covered with glory. The fame of his Odyssey had penetrated not only the quarter where he resided but the whole of artistic Paris; honours were showered upon him, and a famous artist was commissioned to paint his portrait, which was exhibited in the Salon during the forthcoming season. Somewhere among my keepsakes is a picture postcard on which is depicted the old gentleman sitting with a look of radiant happiness on his face, and holding in a close embrace his beloved sarrusophone, the instrument which had played such a picturesque if silent part in the episode.

4
HORNS AND BRASS

HORNS

THE MODERN FRENCH HORN IS LOCATED IN FULL SCORES between the woodwind and the brass, and this is very logical. In many ways it occupies a kind of no-man's-land in this position, having affinities with both wood and brass, yet belonging to neither. In tone it not only blends very well with the woodwind and sounds at times as if it is one of them, but many chamber ensembles—and moments in symphonic works—have been written with this fact in mind. The horn is made either of silver- or copper-alloy, and so appears to be one of the brass instruments, and for practical purposes it is classified as one of the brass department, for the method of blowing the horn is in many ways more similar to the brass approach than to the wood.

The horn comes in that category of instruments known as 'lip reeds'. While all the woodwind instruments except the flute have reeds in their mouthpieces; and while the brass instruments have cup-shaped mouthpieces of various designs but no reeds, the horn has a conical mouthpiece. The player blows in a different way from the rest of the brass by placing his lip against the mouthpiece in order to give the same kind of vibrations to the column of air in the instrument as a reed would do. Although the embouchures for the flute and horn are substantially different, their approach is the same.

The French horn (or merely 'horn' to musicians and consequently never confused with the cor) is a noble instrument. Its sound is at one moment languorous, mellow and rich, equally good in solo as well as in supporting roles; at the next it can be brazen, strident and fierce—quite different.

The origins of the instrument are buried in antiquity. We have only to read of those men in the dark ages of civilisation who blew conches, animals' horns and elephants' tusks to signal to one another. And when that sound turned into more musical sounds, one can imagine how these early men can have been moved by pleasant sensations at their achievement. From these early beginnings came the hunting horns, then later those curly horns used by coachmen as the only means of multiple transport lurched and rolled its way over the potholed dirt tracks from one town to the next. It is a long way between even that kind of horn and the quartet of French horns found today in every symphony orchestra.

The early horns were capable only of uttering the notes of the harmonic series, so unless, when they played with other instruments, they all tuned together, the horns were in the wrong key. The only expedient was to adapt the instrument, like certain of the woodwind department, into different keys, or else to make it possible by mechanical means for it to seem to be pitched in other keys. This was done by providing curved pieces of tubing called *crooks* or straight pieces called *shanks* that could be inserted into the length of the instrument's own tube, either to make it longer (to lower the pitch) or shorter (to raise the pitch).

The French horn is a length of tubing that would reach some eleven feet if it were stretched out straight. The fact that it is coiled round on itself makes no difference at all to the sound. Air blown into it does not mind going round corners when they are completely smooth inside, and when the tube has been so skilfully made that it starts off with a bore of a quarter of an inch and increases absolutely regularly until it arrives at a large bell of between eleven and fourteen inches in diameter. The discovery that crooks and shanks turned a raucous, rural object into a fine and useful musical instrument added greatly to its employment in orchestras, although the system of changing keys was cumbersome in the extreme. Mozart has indicated at least thirty-five such actions during his opera *Don Giovanni*.

Although the horn was introduced into the orchestra around 1757, Bach had given it great opportunities in Germany much earlier. Nevertheless it was a French orchestra which first employed it, and that gave the special, national title to the horn. It was about a hundred years before another way of making it amenable to key change was found, which was by a system of valves, and this became the normal routine among orchestral players. These valves in fact operate in the same way as the

(above) *Brass, showing from left to right, horn, trumpet, trombone, tuba, and euphonium on the floor;* (below) *cymbals and four timpani (one with tuning pedal visible)*

(above) *Reading from left to right, triangle on stand, tubular bells, tam-tam and bass drum;* (below) *vibraphone, celeste, xylophone; and glockenspiel in front, on stand*

crooks did; but by building, as it were, the effects of the crooks into the instrument, and allowing for them to be shut off or brought into the wind channel of the tube, the whole thing became far more manageable. This is why you see a horn player pressing down little pistons, or flat metal tabs, three of them, with the fingers of his left hand. In this way the horn becomes a *chromatic* instrument, that is to say, it can reach every note in the *chromatic scale*, not merely the notes in the harmonic series.

All the same, the horn is by far the most capricious instrument in the whole orchestra. No matter how experienced he is, the chance of a bad note, or 'domino', coming out is very real, and among the world's few virtuoso horn players there is not one who would not agree with this statement. There has been only one exception in living memory and that was Dennis Brain, an unchallenged master of the horn who died far too young in a motor accident.

The orchestral horn of today 'stands' (that is to say, has its natural or home key) in F. So every note in the harmonic series beginning on the F at the bottom of the bass stave, and up to the F at the top of the treble stave, is the compass of the horn before any of the three valves are operated. The double horn goes even further than this. It is coming far more into use now than ten years ago, although the instrument is by no means new. It is, as the name implies, two horns in one, and merely extends the valve idea even further by allowing the player, by means of a fourth valve by his thumb, to short-circuit about three feet of tubing, thus turning it into a B♭ horn by raising its pitch to the fourth above its former F. There have been single B♭ horns, and because they were smaller than the rest they were known as 'short horns'.

Quite by accident a horn player called Hampl in Dresden in 1770 discovered another way altogether of varying the pitch of individual notes. He had received complaints (principally by the strings) about the loudness and coarseness of his newfangled instrument and to appease them he stuffed some wool down the bell. To his great surprise he found that this lowered the pitch by exactly a semitone. This technique, not achieved by wool any longer, but by the right hand, came to be known as *hand-stopping* and as these were the days of the crooks and shanks, it provided the player with a very useful and simple method of obtaining notes outside the harmonic series. Hampl also found that if he put only part of his hand into the bell, the result was as he had originally intended, to muffle the sound, and to affect its quality without altering the pitch. And again by putting the hand further into the bell while blowing, the player can obtain a 'swooping' effect, called a *portamento*, that Benjamin Britten has used in his *Serenade for Tenor, Horn and Strings.*

As yet I have said nothing about the horn's mouthpiece. It is of the utmost importance to the player that he has the right one, which must be compatible and comfortable and fit in with his needs and be an extension of him, just like a good wife. Fig. 7

Fig. 7. Two mouthpieces in section and half true size: horn (left), trumpet (right)

above shows a cross-section drawing of a horn mouthpiece compared with that used in a trumpet; but they vary and for a while a player who is trying out a new one may experience great discomfort and a corresponding deterioration in his performance. To prevent them wearing out, mouthpieces are made from a solid piece of metal, either silver or brass, and are worth examining, for they are works of art.

As you will have gathered, not only does the fact of the horn being in F mean that it is a transposing instrument, but if it is in F and Bb, it is then a double-transposing instrument. When it comes to stopped notes (marked + in the score), the player has to think about them too. Of all instrumentalists, horn players probably need the greatest facility in transposing, but I do not want to labour this point, since it is a knack, when acquired, never forgotten, like riding a horse. The horn is notated in the treble stave and in C. Every sharp and flat is marked where it comes, as if it were always an accidental.

There was a horn session recently when the section of four players were asked to record a short passage from an old score. The parts had been copied by hand and did not indicate in which key the horns were meant to stand. Automatically, I suppose, they took their stand in F, but it wasn't in F at all. 'C' said the principal, and at once and without a moment's hesitation they all mentally readjusted themselves, and out it came at the correct pitch. That is what I mean by a knack.

Horns work in pairs in an orchestra. In Haydn's, Mozart's and the young Beethoven's time, two horns sufficed, but later on they grew to two pairs, sometimes three pairs and even four. The first horn is the principal and takes the higher of two notes while his constant companion the second, takes the lower note. In Italy they consider it discriminatory to number the players, and so each pair is called the corno alto and corno basso respectively. In a four-horn section the 3rd and 4th work together in the same way, with the fourth horn being required, very often, to play very low notes. The higher the notes required, the tighter the lips have to be pursed and pressed against the mouthpiece; and conversely, a player will have to cultivate a loose, flabby lip if he is often going to be needed to play in the very low reaches of the instrument. As a result, should the first horn be away, the third will step-up into his seat, not the second. For concerts with taxing high notes, it is customary for a fifth player to be engaged to relieve the principal of some of the strain. He is always known as the *bumper* horn, or a request will be made for Mr So-and-So to come in and 'bump-up'. The correct name for this is *ripieno* horn, a word that has other meanings in the orchestra, and one which is much deformed in its connotation in the brass band world.

When the Roman city of Pompeii was excavated in 1876, one of the most amazing discoveries, musically speaking, was an instrument called the *tibia* that closely resembled a french horn. Furthermore it had a system of sliders in sleeves, in fact eleven of them, which could be independently operated, so constituting the first, chromatic valve horn to be known, well, on this planet

at any rate. And this device had been lost for seventeen hundred
years.

The brass section consists of trumpets, trombones and often the
tuba too, in a full-strength section, and the number of each
instrument depends on the woodwind and string strength, as
well as, needless to say, the composer's demands. A few other
kinds of instruments occur as well from time to time. The
principal trumpet is considered to be in overall control of the
brass and this is because, like the principal first violin, he is
playing the highest notes and is the one in his section who can be
called upon to give the most brilliant solos and to 'lead' his
section. Trumpets and tubas are related instruments because
they both have valves shaped like pistons. Trombones are entirely different, working on the principal of a sliding device
which is constantly altering the length of the tube. All brass
instruments' notes are based on the harmonic series.

The trumpet is another tube—generally of brass—in which
the air column is set in vibration by the player's lips through a
cup shaped mouthpiece, through which the air passes. The
trumpet's bore is narrow and cylindrical and opens out into a
relatively small bell in the last quarter only of its length. The
modern trumpet is in B♭, although its music is written in C
and it is thus not regarded as transposing. Its compass is from
the F♯ below middle C to the C above the treble stave. The three
valves, when depressed, lower the tone by two, three or one
semitone respectively, and if more than one is depressed, the
number of semitones lower is the sum of those corresponding to
each valve. So in brief, the trumpet is equivalent to six trumpets
in one, or the natural trumpet with six crooks, in one. With
these six different harmonic series at the player's command, it is
a truly chromatic instrument with several ways, towards the
top, of obtaining the same note, and no noticeable deterioration
of tone in a two-octave chromatic scale.

From the time when Joshua's trumpets assisted in bringing
the inhabitants of Jericho rushing to the walls and knocking them
down themselves, the trumpet has been featured and has figured
in archaeological finds and in legend. At the other end of its

history, it figured largely as a masculine instrument in the jazz band, where it shrieked and wailed and strained so hard that a *mute* was found to soften its tone quality and to produce a new effect. The vulgar use of the 'wah-wah' mute and the bowler hat for the same purpose, helped to demolish the trumpet's proper dignity, for like any special effect it becomes debased with repetition. Trumpet mutes used in the orchestral scene are cones of *papier mâché* which are pushed into the bell, but the need for their use is indicated by the composer, not by the player.

The trumpet in D, a smaller instrument, is brighter than the B♭ instrument; the flugelhorn, another member of the family, is in B♭ and has a wider and larger bore and a deeper mouthpiece than its near-relative, the cornet, so that its sound is mellower. It is virtually a keyed bugle.

The cornet is a valved, brass instrument that stands in B♭ and whose natural harmonics exactly fit those of the trumpet. In consequence they can both be played together without fear of any intemperance in pitch. It has descended from the curved, continental posthorn, and is essentially one of them still, but with valves. It has a gently expanding bore but is conical for two thirds of its length, and its mouthpiece is deeper than that of the trumpet. It is broader in tone and is shorter than the trumpet, yet possesses a sound between the horn and the trumpet and with greater flexibility than either. This gives it something of a jaunty character.

I once went past a trumpet player in rehearsal, who had just played a passage on his cornet. I knew it was a cornet but said to him: 'Why don't you try that on the cornet next time? It goes rather well!' He was speechless with amazement, and then assumed that I did not know a trumpet from a cornet, either in sound or appearance.

Trumpet and cornet are sufficiently different in sound for their effects to be marked, but the flugelhorn is not all that very different from the cornet as to mean anything to the general public, especially in heavily scored passages.

One word of warning: should you ever come across an instrument called the trumpet marine, remember that its name extends even further the bounds of lunacy than cor anglais. The trumpet marine is neither a trumpet nor anything to do with dockyards or the seaside. It is a portable *mono-chord* played with a bow. It is very ancient but was not brought to England until the time of the Reformation. It is probably the oldest known bowed instrument.

The next section within the brass is the trombones, by far the oldest instruments in the orchestra to have remained without structural change. They are descended from the Biblical sackbut. While the horns work as a quartet, the trombones come in threes: two tenors and a bass in Britain and America, three tenors in France. The instrument is made of brass, has a cupped mouthpiece and cylindrical bore up to the point where the tube expands and forms the bell. The tenor trombone stands in B♭ and has a total tube length of 107 inches, while the bass instrument in G (as a rule, but occasionally in F) has a total length of 130 inches. Both kinds of instruments are made to three specifications: narrow bore (the 'pea-shooter'), medium bore and large bore. In England it is more common to find medium bore trombones, but in German-speaking countries and in Central Europe, the wide bore is favoured, for it gives great sonority and gravity, a quality which its opponents say is not characteristic of the instrument at all.

A large bore tenor trombone can deal with much of a bass trombone's work as well as its own, making it nearly a dual-purpose instrument. A double-bass trombone is only found in Wagner's scores, and is said to be most exhausting to play because it needs so much breath, and is heavy on the arms.

The trombone mouthpiece is much larger than that of the trumpet family, with a cup that measures one inch across. The exact design is best left to the player's particular preference and requirements. It is, after all, the most individual and personal part of any brass instrument, the part which comes in contact with the player's lips all the time.

A scale is effected by a combination of selecting natural harmonics with lip pressure and also by altering the slide through its seven positions. The tenor's range is from the E below the bass clef to the B♭ above middle C (possibly a little higher with risk attached). The bass trombone starts a minor third lower, at C♯ and its compass extends to the G above middle C. Both instruments' best register is towards the top of the range, and one of the prime examples of superb trombone writing is by Mozart in the 'Tuba Mirum' section of his

Requiem Mass. Wagner and Berlioz also achieve splendid trombone sound: Wagner in the Prelude to Act III of *Lohengrin,* and Berlioz in the Hungarian March from the *Damnation of Faust.*

Bass trombonists read off the bass clef all the time, but tenor players have their parts notated in bass, alto or treble clefs, dependent on the register. The trombone is not a transposing instrument, but the player must be mentally agile to reconcile himself to a constantly changing fundamental note of the harmonic series, since each new position of the slide causes him to be in a different 'harmonic' key, and enables him to be constantly in a position to cover the 'blank' notes in any one series by placing himself in another which will have them as its notes in *that* series. It is possible for a well-written trombone part to have many consecutive notes playable without moving the slide at all; but on the other hand a series of notes upon two semitones at the bottom of the bass clef would call for too rapid movement of the slide from one end of its length to the other to produce the required effect with sufficient accuracy.

'Slide' on a trombone does not mean *glissando,* although the instrument is perfectly capable of that, and of making the rudest sounds possible.

The 'bass trumpet' properly belongs to the trombone part of the brass sections, and in spite of the fact that it looks like a trumpet, it has pistons like a trumpet and is even called a trumpet. It is played with a trombone mouthpiece and is nothing more than a valved trombone, and so it is played by a trombonist, who gets a special fee every time. Wagner, as usual, calls for it in *The Ring.* It reads off the bass clef and is in C.

I said on the previous page that a wide-bore trombone tenor can more or less cover the bass's work for him, but this is unnecessary if a tuba is scored in.

The tuba is the lowest-sounding of all the brass instruments, although the word 'tuba' is subject to misunderstanding. When Wagner was writing *The Ring,* he found that he needed a full consort of eight-plus-one wind instruments like horns. So he used four french horns and then improvised four more of a different nature, a lot deeper, with which he was then able to get an enormously rich and sonorous four-part harmony, with a ninth instrument doubling like the double-bass does in the string section, an octave lower down. The 'new' brand of instruments are still called *Wagner tubas* and are used in all authentic performances of *The Ring*, as well as in several works by Richard Strauss. The ninth instrument *is* what we know as the tuba, more properly described as bass tuba in F. It is also known as the British tuba, and is one of the euphonium family, related to the helicons. Another name for the tuba is its mediaeval one of 'bombardon'.

In Italy, at La Scala Milan, they use an even deeper form of tuba, in B♭ and in America a lower one still in C. The euphonium is a smaller, or tenor version of the tuba (photo facing p. 64) and is known in Germany as the 'baryton'. The B♭ euphonium is a very powerful instrument, very important in brass bands, and is called for under the name of 'tenor tuba' by Strauss, Stravinsky and Gustav Holst.

Helicons are circular forms of this tuba family, of which the only one to be seen in Britain is the sousaphone, an Amerian invention aimed at doing full credit to the marches of the composer who gave the instrument its name. The bell is turned round through 180 degrees to face the same way as the player is looking and ends in a detachable flange of about two feet in diameter. The player has, more or less, to dress himself in his sousaphone by putting it on. He rests one coil on his left shoulder and passes the other under his right arm so that the instrument is coiled all round him. You might have seen Gary Cooper and his sousaphone in the film 'Mr Deeds goes to Town'.

When it comes to punching out tuba notes, it is best done by a sousaphone because the bell of the tuba does not face towards the audience. For a while this instrument had a great vogue with groups in the 1960s, of which the 'Temperance Seven' come first to mind. This was a straight throw forward to the use of the tuba or the sousaphone from Dixieland jazz.

Sidney Torch, the composer and brilliant scorer of 'light music' (much as I detest the epithet), has composed a work called *The London Transport Suite* in which there is a most elegant and well-written solo for a sousaphone. It gambols about in waltz time, emulating an old London Transport omnibus. Otherwise we seldom hear it except in military marches. Stravinsky has brought it out as the dancing bear in *Petrouchka*, in a growling and somewhat frightening way, quite different from the bland omnibus of Sidney Torch.

The sousaphone's and the tuba's part is written in the bass clef and in the key of C. Transposition is automatic and sounding an octave lower than written.

5

TIMPANI, PERCUSSION AND KEYBOARD INSTRUMENTS

TIMPANI

BERLIOZ, THE AUTHOR OF A BOOK ON ORCHESTRATION
that has always remained an authority, was able to play no
orchestral instrument except for the timpani. He was sometimes
to be seen in the pit, whacking away at the great drums, to the
discomfort of other players. He was not a very good timpanist
because he allowed his enthusiasm for the whole work to excite
him out of all proportion to his immediate task on hand.

The timpani, as straightforward drums, are the oldest of all
musical instruments. The cave-man who banged on an animal
skin stretched over a wooden or bone frame had already discovered its principle. But it was not until Tudor times in
England that the instrument became more sophisticated, for
with the introduction of the 'kettledrum', it could be tuned to
about six or seven notes, and what is more, their pitch could be
defined.

The rule today is for three, or possibly four timpani, each
tuned to a different pitch, and read off the bass clef but with a
reminder at the beginning to say how the instruments are to be
tuned. Reading a timpani part is very simple, so far as the pitch
of the notes go, but that is not all there is to it.

Until twenty-five to thirty years ago, the normal method of
tuning was by a series of T-shaped handles round the rim of the
instrument. When a retuning was called for in a score, it was
possible to see the player bending down to listen into the bowl
of the instrument, with a coin in one hand with which he tapped
the 'head' while his other hand adjusted the handles which either
tightened or slackened the membrane. Nowadays timps are
tuned by a pedal which does this mechanically, and it is also

possible for a player to allow the sound to be heard of the head being stretched or relaxed, when a curious, eerie, wailing murmur emerges from it. The science and use of different sticks with hard or soft heads is an interesting one, but cannot be gone into here; suffice it to say that a player can—or if the composer says so, he must—change the type of stick he uses so as to achieve the best possible effect according to the mood of the music being played. Drums and trumpets have always gone together in military music and indeed there is nothing better than a drum to reinforce the trumpet sound at a climax. Normally the timpani player concentrates upon his three (or four) instruments to the exclusion of any others. For while he may not be playing all the time, he is very likely counting the bars until his next entrance. The kind of information which a timpani part gives a player is shown here below, and counting the 'empty'

Fig. 8. Extract from a timpani part showing many bars' rest

bars is an art which even the most musical people are unable to do without practise, as the following story will show. The great conductor, Hans von Bülow, and his pupil and assistant Richard Strauss, were together in Meiningen in the year 1885, where the orchestra was going to have the honour of playing the first performance of Brahm's Fourth Symphony under Bülow's direction. They also played the *Academic Festival Overture* in which, so as to avoid the expense of engaging extra players, Bülow took the cymbals and Strauss the bass drum. Brahms conducted. It was evidently a poor idea to cheesepare on the extras, for neither Bülow nor Strauss was able to count rests or empty bars. Strauss lost himself after the fourth bar but managed to get hold of a score (a full score) and followed from that. Bülow kept going over to one of the trumpeters to find out where they were, started to recount, got lost, and repeated the procedure.

Fig. 9 shows four lines from the combined bass drum and cymbals part of Brahms's *Academic Festival Overture*, which so confounded the two great musicians. There is one timpani player in London who treats his instruments (and they are his own too) as if they were his children. Nobody is allowed to

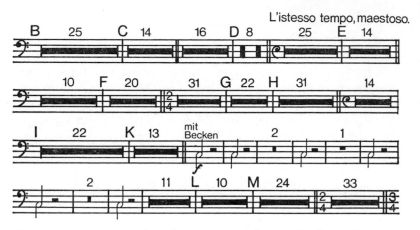

Fig. 9. Extract from a bass drum and cymbal part (Brahms's Academic Festival Overture)

touch them without wearing gloves, and the attendants at concert halls where he goes hate moving his gear at any time because he is so particular. Mind you, the highly polished, copper bowls of these timpani really do look splendid. He wears gloves himself, white ones, except during performances, and seems to be wrapped up in this love-affair with his glorious instruments. But on account of their size it is difficult to rehearse with them often enough, and so this player makes the best of a bad job by having a long 'warm-up' in the concert hall where the performance is to take place, and right up to the half hour beforehand, when the audience start to come in. But the fuss he makes about being stopped!

In most places it is considered to be in very bad taste for any player to be 'discovered' (in the theatrical sense) on the platform when the audience arrive, and I was most surprised in 1972 at the Royal Festival Hall to see a gaggle of players in full view and industriously scraping away. They were the complete double bass section of the Berlin Philharmonic Orchestra, getting round a particularly awkward phrase from Beethoven's 'Pastoral' Symphony under the direction of their principal. I could not help thinking that it was more of a show-off than a necessity.

But to return to the timpanist. His job is by no means as easy as it looks, for he has to be completely accurate in his intonation and if possible he should have perfect pitch. He must also be absolutely precise in the manner in which he plays, because one can scarcely conceal the sound of timpani which come in at the wrong place. A player who is not possessed of a good ear and an unshakeable sense of rhythm and tempo is unlikely to get very far in the profession.

PERCUSSION

The word 'percussion' means to an orchestral musician the man who is in charge of all those peculiar bits-and-pieces and odds-and-ends which so often are not strictly musical, but border on sound effects. But today, in the era of the 'new music', the demands for tiny gradations of weird sound qualities, produced by whatever means the ingenious mind can devise, are happening all the time, and an even greater assortment of kitchen equipment has been seen on the stand.

The late Constant Lambert wrote a fascinating composition called *The Rio Grande*. Its instrumentation is most unusual:

0.0.0.0. 0.2. 2 cnts. 3.1. perc(5). Piano Mixed Ch. Str.

This means: no woodwind at all. No horns. 2 trumpets and 2 cornets, three trombones and a tuba. Timpani, 4 percussion players, a piano, mixed chorus and strings. Lambert elaborates his percussion requirements in the score, which curiously does not pick out the timpanist although he is required, as the detailed notes tell us. Have a look at the score of *The Rio Grande* and then listen to a record of it. See if you can pick out the various percussion instruments, some of which are not often heard.

The piano in this work is used percussively, and not as the melodic or romantic instrument which we know from Grieg, Schumann or Tchaikovsky. After all, a piano's action is percussive, as Stravinsky knew very well. Its use in *Petrouchka* is an example, and today's composers have followed him to an even greater extent.

Here are the names and brief descriptions of some of the most commonly found percussion instruments, to show the range of intention and of effect behind them, and starting with *untuned* percussion (that is to say instruments which do not make a definite pitched note, just a sound).

Side Drum. This is a small instrument with a parchment head on both ends, and with a 'snare' or length of wire to and fro four or five times across one end. When the drum is beaten with thin wooden sticks, the snare vibrates as well as the head, producing a very hard and dry sound. When played on the opposite end, the one without snares, the typically muffled effect of a funeral drum is achieved, both sinister and imposing. The technique of beating a roll on a side drum with two sticks takes nearly a year to acquire, and is then a most impressive accomplishment. Some good examples of a side drum roll are to be found in Rossini's Overture *La gazza Ladra*; between the scenes of Stravinsky's *Petrouchka*, where the player has to keep it going while the scenery is being changed, and at the opening of the Gipsy Dance from Rimsky-Korsakov's *Capriccio Espagnol*, where unwary listeners leap to their feet, taking it for the British National Anthem!

Bass Drum. This is the largest drum in use. When Toscanini came to London in 1937, he insisted that an especially large bass drum be made for use in his performance of Verdi's *Requiem*; and although this one no longer exists, having been destroyed during the war, the BBC own another, still called the 'Toscanini Drum', which is not only used for the *Requiem*, but also for the *1812 Overture* of Tchaikovsky. Either beaten, with a special, soft-headed stick; or rolled; or whacked (but with care and not by bandsmen please, who have been known to put the stick right through it), it is capable of the effects of thunder, cannonfire, or can sound ominous and threatening when played softly. Occasionally a double-headed stick is used. Of all percussion instruments, the bass drum best lives up to Cecil Forsyth's opinion that 'its principal effect is its entry'.

Anvil. This is exactly what it says it is, but on a small scale. There used to be at Queen's Hall in London a full-size one, but its weight was a great disadvantage. When struck, it produces a penetrating clink, with a dull sensation afterwards. Verdi made great use of it in his 'Anvil Chorus' from *Il Trovatore*, while Wagner calls for eighteen anvils in *Das Rheingold*, to be played offstage. His demands, in this case, are never met.

Castanets are an old Spanish device of two small and hollow pieces of shaped wood, designed to be fitted over two fingers, and struck together while the person concerned is dancing. The orchestral percussion player does not resort to these antics (as a rule) because he has a hinged pair of castanets fixed to a block, which he operates mechanically with one hand, while he might shake a tambourine with the other.

Crotales are a variation of the castanets, and are made either of wood or metal. They are still more ancient, being portrayed in Egyptian wall pictures.

Cymbals. Otherwise known as 'clashpans'. They can either be, literally, clashed together in front of the player's face, often with a great flourish, and certainly with a fine edge to a climax; or suspended and beaten with a soft-headed drumstick; or else they can be fixed together on to a vertical attachment (called a 'high-hat') and brought together by a pedal, as in dance bands. Alternatively their edges can be rubbed together to produce a sizzling effect.

Gong or Tam-tam. This scarcely needs description, but is a large, circular metal dish, with the edge upturned all round. It is struck with a soft-headed beater. The gong is a very ancient instrument, originating in China, and all the best gongs still come from the East. Tchaikovsky uses it to great effect twice, first in his Fantasie-Overture *Hamlet*, where it makes a *sf* entrance about a quarter of the way through; and in the *Sixth Symphony*, near the end, where its single, muffled entry is depressing in the extreme.

Tambourine is another instrument of antiquity. It is known to have been used, in more or less the same form as we have it today, by the Romans. It consists of a narrow wooden hoop covered on one side with parchment like a small drum (it is about twelve inches in diameter). In addition it has small circular metal plates, or 'jingles', attached to the edge of the hoop so that they rattle, not only when the tambourine is moved, but also when it is struck, when they vibrate sympathetically. The tambourine can be played either by shaking it in the air, by banging the parchment with the knuckles, or by rubbing it with the thumb.

Triangle. This is the smallest instrument in the whole orchestra and is by far the simplest. Its shape gives it its name, and the thin steel rod with three sides has its two ends open and not touching. It is struck with a small metal rod, and then shows its peculiar properties. It never sounds out of tune no matter what is being played, because it absorbs harmonies round it and seems never to utter a discordant note itself. Liszt made emphatic use of the triangle in his *First Piano Concerto*, where it has a solo part, so much so as to give the work the nickname of 'The Infernal Triangle'.

Thundersheet. This is really a theatrical device, but again required by Strauss in his *Alpine Symphony*, to simulate the obvious background to his already terrific musical storm. The unfortunate player who is assigned to the thundersheet in this work will leave the concert hall with aching arms, because it goes on remorselessly, and so far as it seems to him, endlessly.

Wind Machine. This is another adjunct to natural effects. It is a cylinder, mounted horizontally on a stand in such a way that it can be rotated by means of a handle. The sides of the cylinder are slatted, and these slats come into close contact with a stretched piece of silk or canvas. According to how rapidly the handle is turned and the cylinder goes round, the whistling effect so achieved will become higher and shriller. Vaughan Williams put the wind machine to most effective use in his *Sinfonia Antartica*.

Malcolm Arnold has composed a comic work called *A Grand, Grand Overture* in which there are requirements for four rifle shots, an electric floor-polisher, and three vacuum cleaners. All these 'musical instruments' are played by percussionists, and they have to be Union members. It is a highly amusing sight to watch them, especially as the floor-polisher has a habit of running away with its 'player'. What Arnold was after, apart from the spectacle that he devised for one of Hoffnung's 'Interplanetary Festivals', was the whirring sound of the domestic instruments that have the sound of gentle harmonics if you are unaware of their source. The rifle shots were merely a diversion. A licence is needed for these too, although they only fire blanks.

There is another category of percussion instruments, which may seem almost comical, and indeed they often figure in humorous compositions. The *Rattle* is the same, horrible instrument which is used in profusion at football matches, but without tact or subtlety under those circumstances. Strauss calls for one in his *Till Eulenspiegel*.

These are by no means all the instruments which a percussion player may find himself having to handle, but they are probably quite enough for normal, and a few abnormal purposes.

Bells. Normal orchestral bells are metal tubes cut to lengths so as to provide approximately pitched notes of about an octave, round about the middle of the piano range. I say 'approximately' because they are seldom in tune. They are suspended in a frame, where they can vibrate after being struck close to the top with a hammer, but because their harmonics are so rich, they often give the effect of not being in tune, which is just as bad as being out of tune to start with. They are normally provided in a diatonic scale of E♭. Apart from simulating the sound of church bells, which they do badly, because they are pitched too high, two deep bells, C and G in the bass, are needed for Berlioz's *Symphonie Fantastique*. When Pierre Boulez was recording this work with the London Symphony Orchestra, he insisted upon getting plate bells from Eastern Europe, the only place where they are still made. When one realises that a proper bell that sounds middle C would weigh more than twenty tons, it is clear that some sort of simulation is called for. Plate bells come nearer than tubular bells to an authentic sound of steeple bells; the only alternative is a tape recording of real bells, such as they use at Covent Garden in London during performances of

Moussorgsky's *Boris Godunov*. But in the concert hall this is not to be encouraged.

Glockenspiel. There are two kinds of *Glockenspiel* (meaning, in German, 'Bell-play') one with keys and one without. The latter is constructed of steel plates that are mounted on a stand and are hit with two small hammers to produce a bright and bell-like sound It is similar in construction to the xylophone.

Xylophone. This has bars of wood instead of metal plates, and the sound is more clunky. The resonators are hit with spoon-shaped beaters. Saint-Saëns scores it into his *Danse Macabre* to give the effect of rattling bones, but it has other, more cheerful uses.

Vibraphone, very much in evidence nowadays in conjunction with the 'new music'. It is cousin to the 'Glock' but has metal tubes hanging perpendicularly under each bar which, when set into vibration by electricity, produces a cloudy and ethereal version of the sound peculiar to this genre of instrument. Since the 'vibes' are plugged into the mains in order to get the machinery going which causes the vibrancy, it is always as well if the particular player stands on a rubber mat when he addresses the machine.

Harp. A very noble instrument which might be thought to belong to the strings, but which is attached for all purposes to the percussion department, although it is important enough to deserve its own entry in every instrumentation in which it appears.

It is possibly the most elegant looking instrument in the orchestra, although there will be those who disagree, standing alone with its decorated pillar and graceful curve of the neck, resembling almost exactly those instruments which the Egyptians used as long ago as the thirteenth century BC. The modern 'double-action' harp has seven foot-pedals, each of which can tighten or slacken every same note in each of the harp's six and a half octaves The instrument is treated as being in the key of C♭, and when the pedals are all depressed one notch, it is in C major; when they are pressed again into the second notch, the harp is in C♯ major A harpist uses both hands, either to twang the strings individually and to bring out a melody, or else to produce that inimitable *glissando* of swirling upward or downward cascades of fluent, flowing sound, referred to in the orchestra as 'knitting'. By touching strings with the inside of the wrist as they are played, it is possible for the harpist to get the harmonic an octave higher, and such notes are indicated in the part with a small circle over them. Mozart wrote a *Flute and Harp Concerto*; Berlioz gave it an important part in the second movement of the *Symphonie Fantastique*; and so did Tchaikovsky, of course in *Swan Lake*. Debussy, too, made excellent and evocative use of the instrument. One odd thing about harp playing is that the instrumentalist never needs to use the little fingers.

It is more common for harp players to be women. Apart from Osian Ellis, who is a virtuoso, there is only one other man in a London orchestra and one or two others on the fringe.

KEYBOARD INSTRUMENTS

This section includes the normal keyboard instruments, such as the organ and the solo piano, as well as the keyed percussion instruments that occasionally have the same name as those in the previous section and which are activated by means of hammers or other strikers.

Keyed Glockenspiel looks like a silent practice keyboard such as pianists take with them on their travels. It is used for Papageno's bells in Mozart's *Magic Flute* and has a very bright, clean sound. Its compass is from C above middle C for three octaves.

Celeste (properly celesta) was invented in 1886 in Paris by Victor Mustel. Its first known use was by Tchaikovsky in the 'Danse de la Fée Dragée' in *Casse Noisette*. Story has it that the composer had an instrument secretly taken to St Petersburg for the première of his ballet at Christmas-time 1892, but it seems strange that no previous use should have been put to the instrument within six years. Richard Strauss makes effective use of the celesta in *Der Rosenkavalier* which, when coupled with its own bitter harmonies, presents a musical question-mark. This is the only keyed instrument that never needs tuning. The keys operate hammers which strike small metal bars, and these are permanently installed.

Piano. As already described, the piano may frequently be used as a percussion instrument, and possibly Stravinsky has made more use of it in this manner than any other composer. But otherwise its use is too familiar to need emphasis. Until the present century, the only place for a piano on the platform with a symphony orchestra was as the solo instrument in a concerto. It might be found in the orchestra pit taking the place of the harpsichord to accompany recitative in opera, but that use is anachronistic, even though the late Fritz Busch saw no objection to it at Glyndebourne in England before the last war. In Richard Strauss's opera, *Ariadne auf Naxos* (see Fig. 10, p. 85), the piano is used both percussively and also to accompany a solo singer. But the use of a piano with an orchestra, merely to thicken the sound or add a different colouring, is usually weak and ineffectual unless the other instruments are playing quietly.

Harpsichord. The family of which this is a member also includes the *virginal* and the *spinet*. Only very occasionally, and generally for an effect, do we see a harpsichord on the concert platform, unless a baroque group is playing for example Bach or Scarlatti in as authentic a manner as possible. The harpsichord's tone is rather thin, operating by plucking at strings whereas the piano action hammers them. It cannot possibly compete in volume with an orchestra.

Organ. Handel's organ concertos are still played, and of course there is no question of the 'king of instruments' being drowned by even the largest orchestra. All the major concert halls have good pipe organs and the blend of string sound from the orchestra and the organ's all-wind sound together, is often very rewarding. Orchestral wind instruments and the organ have little to say to one another. William Walton has made use of the organ in building up to a climax in his *Belshazzar's Feast*, while Strauss does the same at the beginning of his *Also Sprach Zarathustra,* and leaves the organ playing alone to end the first section. Strauss's *Festival Prelude* for organ and large orchestra

Fig. 10. Page of full score divided into two 'systems' and showing the piano part as semi-percussive

is a bombastic, though exciting work, not very often performed.

Harmonium. This instrument, for so long associated with Moody and Sankey, and the 'straightening out' of interesting and original native harmonies by the missionaries, is sometimes found on an orchestral platform to give a special, thickening effect to the texture. It belongs to the reed-organ family, and not to the organ proper, which is constructed of whistle-pipes. Other members of the reed-organ family are the *mouth-organ,* the *accordion* and the *concertina.* Up to only a short while ago one would scarcely expect to find a mouth-organ with an orchestra, but Vaughan Williams (and others) have dignified the instrument with a concerto. When it is played by such an artist as Larry Adler or Tommy Reilly (whose *harmonicas,* as they call them, are made of solid silver) it is truly dignified, and I mention it as the final word on the whole orchestra.

6

CONDUCTORS

CONDUCTORS CAME INTO THEIR OWN WHEN THE SIZE OF the orchestra grew from a chamber group, when control was easy, to its often present proportions, when it requires all the efforts and skill of one man (women conductors are rare) so placed that he can see all the players and they can all see him. The audience can also see him as well, and quite often they either cannot see anybody else, or are so bemused by his antics that they do not want to look elsewhere. He is by far the most extrovert person in sight, even if there is a soloist, and one might wonder why he carries on in the way that he does. It has been said: 'The Conductor is the artist; the musicians are the craftsmen'. Many conductors would dispute that by arguing that he is too far removed from the making of the sound, and that the musicians do it all. Other conductors would agree whole-heartedly.

The conductor is there, on the rostrum (or the 'box') in a three-fold capacity. Firstly, he will have had a hand in 'building' the programme which he is to conduct, and in giving his advice about it, as part of the season's contribution of planned concerts. Secondly he will have thoroughly studied the scores of each work, will have stipulated the number of players he requires if there is any doubt, and will have discussed any vexing points with the leader and any section principal directly concerned. And lastly, when he gets up on to the box to take the first rehearsal, he must inspire and encourage the orchestra as they play. After all, they can, after a fashion, play without him.

Yet there must be no sense of strain, of awkwardness, least of all any impression by the orchestra that they do not worship the conductor any less than his fans in the audience. So it is that the majority of orchestras exercise this convention and give no indication of their views of the man on the box. At the beginning of the concert when he comes on, he has already been given a 'build-up' by the leader, whose entrance is the prelude to the star of the evening, the conductor himself. When the leader walks on he expects applause, and then joins the seated orchestra. From then on they watch the leader for a cue to rise as a token of esteem and ordinary politeness when the conductor walks on to the platform or—in the case of Georg Solti—half-runs on. Again, at the end of the concert, when the conductor urges the orchestra to rise and accept part of the applause with him, it is the leader who decides how many times (or even whether) they shall do so. A well disciplined orchestra will rise together and will look pleased. It is not only the conductor who has to act. I know of only one orchestra which behaves differently. They stand for their leader when he comes on and remain implacably seated, no matter who the conductor is, once the leader has taken his seat. So you have the odd appearance of an orchestra sitting down, rather than standing up, as the conductor comes on.

By playing with the conductor and *for* the conductor—and this is the ideal—the players submit to his discipline. How they do this, whether they even realise they are doing it, and how the conductor is able to achieve it—herein lie all the secrets of good, bad or indifferent conductors, and anything less than good is bad. Since music is a highly organised art, so organised that it approaches mathematics and a science, there is no need to suppose that it is self-supporting or self-generating, once the players have begun. The fact that they are working towards a performance implies that, in the professional sense, it must not stop once it has begun, and that it must be put over to the audience without histrionics or any impression that it is difficult. In order to achieve this, all those on the platform, including the conductor, must subordinate themselves to the music. They must also attempt to make themselves inconspicuous, visually speaking, although this cannot entirely apply to the conductor, nor to a soloist. And yet the best kind of discipline which a conductor can achieve is one whereby he channels all the audience's senses into sound, and makes them oblivious to anything else. That requires considerable ability.

Many of the ways in which this can ultimately be done are worked out and settled at rehearsals. There should never be an audience at an early rehearsal—some conductors refuse admis-

sion at all rehearsals. Everybody on the platform is concerned in
a workshop activity, rough-hewing the music, planing it down,
shaping it and polishing it, fitting it together so that the joins
never show. It is unfair to composer, conductor and players if
this arduous, long-winded and often uninteresting process is
observed. And it can be uninteresting after constant repetition of
a phrase. Admittedly the thought of attending a rehearsal might
appeal to some people: it almost borders on voyeurism, for it is
watching the forbidden. But it can be unfair to players who are
repeatedly—or even once is enough—stopped or criticised or
otherwise made to appear smaller than they really are. And not
a few conductors are given to picking on one player constantly,
making him or her the whipping boy for the whole orchestra.

Rehearsals can be far more exhausting than the actual performance because the atmosphere is likely to be more highly
charged—with a taxing conductor, especially. He has to be far
more in evidence than 'on the night', guiding, advising, stopping
and repeating, talking, even shouting, perhaps never stopping
at all (within the limits laid down by the union) until the very
last minute, when he has to be reminded that his time is—at
last—up. And then he may not be satisfied. Georg Solti has
possibly the most unusual and exhausting procedure at his
rehearsals. He gives what amounts to a 'talk-down' (as from
flying control to an airline pilot). He announces a little before
each event in the score what he wants, briefing each section or
individual player, stressing time changes, dynamics, *rallentandos*
or *accelerandos*, emphasising in words what his stick and his
eyes will alone be able to convey during the performance. It is a
positively wearing experience even to witness one of these
glowing and living commentaries on the music. It is one way of
doing it. But most players hate it. They are unable to concentrate on their own task with that rather staccato and high-
pitched not to say hectic voice going on for nearly three hours.

At the performance there must be no impression whatsoever
of anything like this, anything upsetting or troublesome or
brain-fatiguing. The only impression must be of quiet confidence
on everybody's part, and on the part of the conductor especially.
If he comes on to the platform with a smile and looks pleasantly
at the audience, he will have made a good start. Then he should
give a visible smile to the orchestra, possibly a nod to one or

two of them as if to say 'Yes, I know you have a moment or two
to come, but don't worry, I shall be there when you need me'. A
short second's pause on the rostrum gives everybody the feeling
of confidence in the conductor before he raises his arms, nods to
the leader and begins. Very often too, he will give a quick shake
of the leader's hand as he comes past him: the firm shake is to
come later.

All this will set a most favourable scene. It may smack of a
ritual, but is not all concert-going that? And in any case people
like rituals, they are most comforting. On the other hand a conductor who dispenses with this ritualistic behaviour can do
damage to the whole concert. If he comes on looking sulky or
gloomy or angry, nobody warms to him. If he ignores the
orchestra there is at once a feeling that something is wrong; and
if he whispers to a player, nobody in the audience can hear what
he is saying, and there is nothing more calculated to give rise to
speculation.

In fact the conductor may be torturing himself with doubts
and fears, but he should never show them. He must give the impression, even if it is only that, of being perfectly confident of the
success of the evening's concert, and that of all people present, he
is going to enjoy it the most. Yet inside, he may be thinking of
that partly mis-spent rehearsal, of the whole section that he re-
hearsed insufficiently, of the second movement which he did not
properly shape. Many a conductor, after a bad performance, has
been unable to face anybody and has slunk off alone, to dwell on
the misery which he has brought upon himself.

The conductor is, after all, solely responsible for the way
things go, even if accidents happen. He is the driver of the
vehicle which is the orchestra, and if it becomes involved in a
crash, well, he is going to be the one who loses his licence, his
reputation. And it is not only the way in which he guides the
vehicle safely home, but also the manner in which he does so.
And musically speaking, this manner can probably be best
described as two things: balance and interpretation.

Balance means the exact amount of volume and kind of tone
which each element of the orchestra is required to provide at any
given moment, yet always, in effect, changing. Without skilful
and experienced handling of a score, the slightest alteration of,
say, the volume of a timpani roll or of a trumpet's blast to more

than the required level would entirely obliterate a telling phrase on the violas; and it is the understanding by the conductor of the need for complete plasticity of sound and the ability to achieve it which results in a clear and musically credible performance. A player may not understand why he is being so savagely hushed, and he may resent it. But if he were standing in the place of the conductor, or audience, he would appreciate that it is not a trombone concerto after all. His instrument has a place in the whole scheme of sound, but not *double forte* all the time.

Some conductors fancy their powers of hearing and say that they are able to detect a false note anywhere. This is patently ridiculous, especially in *tutti* passages. It is much safer, if the conductor is in doubt, for him to ask the section in question to play that bit again while the rest of the orchestra is *tacet*. This will expose them to their own disadvantage if they play it again incorrectly, and then there is real cause to put it right.

So a good conductor is one who not only secures the goodwill of the orchestra, but one who is able to obtain a reading at rehearsal that achieves the right balance. After that, imperceptibly at first during rehearsals, but within his own mind, comes the interpretation. This is often impossible for the listener to disentangle from the sheer gestatory sound at rehearsal, because it is the last layer of creative activity on the conductor's part. It is the gloss which he gives to the finished work, the personal touch which either does or does not crown the whole and leaves the audience exhausted, dumbfounded, exhilarated, ecstatic—or else sends them out feeling nothing at all. And that last effort is the hallmark of failure, even though some of them may not even be musical people. For great music in the hands of even the most run-of-the-mill conductor has got to say *something*.

A conductor may have scaled his rehearsals beautifully, have led up and eventually screwed up the players to the requisite state to give a stunning performance, only to be unable to impose a reading on the programme that was in any way memorable, novel, or even interesting. In other words, poor fellow, he had not been able to invest any of the works with an interpretation. It didn't mean anything, he had not conveyed the composer's intentions to anybody.

Audience reaction and participation is a vital element in a performance, and within this two-way arrangement, some understanding and sympathy on the part of the listeners is always implied. Unfortunately too many conductors take it for granted that every single person who has paid to come in will be familiar with the works that are being played, and that they will consequently appreciate every little nuance or quirk of playing and interpretation. There are very likely, at every single concert anywhere, several people who have never before heard one of the works being played. Here is a remarkable, invisible and unknown link between three persons: the listener, the conductor and the composer And it is the conductor, in the middle, who has the unique opportunity of planting in this listener's mind, now and for ever, the yardstick by which every future performance of this work will be judged. He may even have cultivated, by this one performance, a lifelong admirer, within which state exists loyalty and gratitude.

One does find members of an audience who have absolutely no idea at all of what they are meant to be hearing, no idea of what they are supposed to be registering. It needs somebody to start the laughter when it is a humorous work, or another to start the applause immediately the work is over. Spontaneity is vital. No effort on the conductor's part can possibly do more than help catch up his duffers among the audience in the general enthusiasm which is being felt by the others. The story is told of a couple of women at the old Crystal Palace in London, where the building's acoustics were so perfect as to be positively embarrassing if abused. In a moment's pause in a hushed and wrapt oratorio, one female said to another: 'We always fry ours in lard'. This rang round the whole concert hall in a stentorian whisper.

But this is not the worst assault that has been made upon conductors. Several have, at one time or another, been shot at. And many a musician feels that this practice should be more frequently observed in certain quarters. For more often than not, conductors are held in some contempt, if not in sheer dislike by seasoned players. Most of all these men dislike the conductor who spends a great deal of time in polishing his efforts, in creating and establishing slight changes to what has become established as 'right', and in using up every available minute at rehearsals. For a conductor to go to 'the last knockings' will be regarded as a poor effort on his part. So far as the musicians are concerned, it is they who are heard, they who will determine whether the concert is to succeed or not, they who have done all the hard work beforehand while 'he just stands up there, making a nuisance of himself'. Of course this is a one-eyed way of looking at things. No single musician, with the possible exception of the leader (whose ears and eyes and intellect have to stretch further than the few cubic feet of air which he occupies) is fully aware of a good conductor's intentions. One conductor may attack a certain phrase in one way, while another conductor may have entirely different views. They may both be right, each in his own way, but musicians can hardly ever appreciate this, and so far as they are concerned, the conductor is up there to make life difficult, if not intolerable for them. With this in mind, it is more than necessary for a conductor to be something of a psychologist.

You may ask whether a conductor is really necessary. For a programme of symphonic works, the answer is undoubtedly *Yes*. The forces are too large, the music often too complicated to expect ninety-odd people to find their way right through the score without mishap. There can, after all, be mishaps *with* a conductor. It is not as if the score contains complete directions for a complete performance; it is only a guide, like a map of the terrain to be covered. And if you consider that there is no direct road across it, a guide's assistance is invaluable. And this is what the conductor has got to be: a guide. Stravinsky was often content to stand back, even to stop beating time when his orchestra was doing all right. He did not relax one scrap, but watched and listened. At the first, faintly doubtful suggestion he was there again, right on top of them all, pulling things back into place.

If there is nobody to take a firm stand when things are going wrong, to insist that they are 'Three before 106' or whatever it is (a direct reference to a place in the score meaning 3 bars before the figure 106 which everybody has marked) the resulting total collapse of the orchestra is not as funny as it might seem.

In the case of groups smaller than a full orchestra, there is a far closer physical and mental approach between the players and their acknowledged leader. This can, in fact, be the orchestral leader, but more often it is a keyboard player. Everybody can look to him for the start, and after that he can be relied on to pick up a flagging beat. Very occasionally one can today hear a performance of a piano concerto, usually by Mozart or the early Beethoven, in which the soloist is also the conductor, the same idea. Daniel Barenboim is known to perform this double act, and Edwin Fischer used to do the same. But one wonders how the soloist can be at the same time an individual player and still have an ear and a sympathy for the last desk of violins, especially when he has his back to them.

Without going further into the means at a conductor's disposal for asserting his interpretation on a composition, let us mention some of the conductors who have been the most loyal and not so loyal interpreters of the great compositions in the repertoire. Above all, Toscanini was always completely faithful to the composer's intentions. He was rude beyond belief; his English was elementary and he larded his monologues and tirades with Italian epithets, for at the end of his life he worked entirely in the United States. He was so impatient of mistakes that he used to set the players' nerves on edge, but from their point of view the worst of it all was that he had a photographic memory and knew every note that each player had in front of him. Toscanini was always right. He had it engraved indellibly on his mind, exactly as the composer had wished it. Not one dotted quaver was out of place, not one unexpected accidental in a violin run. His orchestra, the NBC Symphony, died with him, and that in itself shows what immense control and personality Toscanini exerted over it.

The Wagnerian tenor, Lauritz Melchior, once told a good story about Toscanini and his memory. The Italian was conducting at Bayreuth in 1933 and during an early rehearsal of *Tannhäuser*, with piano, had occasion to stop the pianist and tell him to be careful about what he played. The man was puzzled and asked what Toscanini meant. 'The bottom B♭ of course' replied Toscanini, 'you played a B♮.' The pianist replied that he had a B♮ in the piano score. 'I say it should be a B♭', insisted Toscanini, 'it is played by the second bassoon'. Somebody went to fetch the full score and when it arrived Toscanini was perfectly right, the second bassoon had indeed got an important B♭ at exactly that bar, not a B♮. Even in a piano reduction the maestro had recognised not only a mistake, but exactly where the mistake occurred, and for thirty-five years it had gone unnoticed. Such extra-sensory musicianship is most exceptional, and might have come to Toscanini by way of exchange for the loss of his near sight.

Toscanini was heartily disliked by a lot of musicians, especially in America. There is a story of a little violinist who went to the office of Toscanini's orchestra a month after the great conductor had died, to ask for a ticket to the memorial service. He was told, in some surprise, that all tickets had been disposed of weeks before. 'Oh well,' said the little man, 'save me one for Szell's then'.

George Szell, born Georg Széll in Budapest in 1897, was a child prodigy on the piano and then took up conducting with great success. His fidelity to the score and to the composer's intentions was without compromise, and as he had been a practising musician from an early age, he had come to absorb more sheer skills and capacities than others who came more slowly to the profession. As a result, Szell was never beaten in argument because he had such an enormous fund of musical knowledge, some half-forgotten, which came to the surface when needed. He was super-meticulous, always checked and double-checked facts, and was one of the best prepared conductors on the rostrum. At the same time he was not above seeking views or confirmation from players over something which concerned them directly, so from this point of view he could be generous and far-thinking. Yet overall he was a martinet, as we shall find out later.

Sir Henry Wood was another faithful disciple of the composer, whose bluff exterior gave more of the impression of a country squire than of a musician. Known to all musicians as 'Timber', he had one very estimable idiosyncrasy. He insisted on absolute punctuality. His huge pocket watch sat on the desk throughout rehearsals and he began as soon as it said so. And woe betide any player who came in late, because in those days, before the war, he could very properly be fined. 'Timber's' rehearsals, by the same token, always ended exactly on the dot too, even in the middle of a movement or a phrase. He put down his baton and that was the end.

There are other conductors who may be said to come under the category of liberal in their attitude to the score, and by liberal I mean sensibly elastic. Otto Klemperer, who died in 1973 at the great age of 87, was reputed to take slower and slower tempi with each advancing year. But as the world gets older it also gets faster: everything is screwed up tighter including musical pitch. Klemperer went into reverse. His Wagner still possessed the 'Bayreuth beat', that deliberate tempo which, it is said, was handed down from Richard Wagner himself. The last two exponents of this tradition, one who worked at Bayreuth and the other who has not, are the late Hans Knappertsbusch and Reginald Goodall. This is not the place to dwell upon the relative merits and demerits of slow or fast tempi taken to extremes, but as Gustav Mahler remarked: *'Tradition ist Schlamperei.'* That is to say, 'tradition means slovenliness'. That was in Vienna in 1897. Today in Vienna the slogan, when applied to the opera, is *Schlamperei ist Tradition.*

Leonard Bernstein, for long associated with the New York Philharmonic Symphony Orchestra, conductor of opera at the Metropolitan, and of symphony concerts all over the world, is also, of course, a composer. This does not mean that he conducts his own works exclusively, far from it. But to European ears he is given to far too many excesses of emotion, that cause him to overstep the bounds of propriety, yet for all the best reasons on his side. He is a man profoundly dedicated to music, but does not seem quite to know when to turn off the emotion and let the music do the rest.

Among living conductors, Herbert von Karajan can scarcely ever be accused of perpetrating a musical solecism, especially as he is something of an expert in the music of the three conductors who mainly provide his circumscribed repertoire: Mozart, Beethoven and Richard Strauss. He is scrupulous about his choice of tempi and dynamics, never offends the purists, and with the Berlin Philharmonic Orchestra at his command he never fails to produce a very exciting concert. But although it is occasionally present in his music, there is one commodity which is never seen on his face: a smile. He is too much in deadly earnest for it to allow him to appear just slightly human for once, and that is a pity. He is a superman in every respect, and in consequence never lets us forget that he is removed from us mortals by the distance of his bodyguard, his manager, his lawyer and his aeroplane (which he pilots himself).

Akin to von Karajan in niceties of interpretation, though very

Four musical knights: (above) *Sir Henry Wood* (left) *and Sir Adrian Boult* (right); (below) *Sir Thomas Beecham, Bt.* (left) *and Sir Malcolm Sargent* (right)

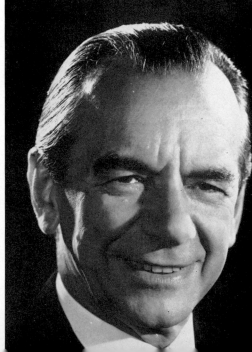

Four great European conductors: (above) *Arturo Toscanini* (left) *and Wilhelm Furtwängler* (right); (below) *Sir Georg Solti* (left) *and Herbert von Karajan* (right)

different in personality, is Eugene Ormandy, conductor of the Philadelphia Orchestra since 1941, and associate conductor for three years earlier than that. He is a lovable man while Karajan is cold; Ormandy is full of fun and tends to gambol about like a little bear. He can be strict on the box, but always generous and warm-hearted.

A recently arrived star on the London scene, André Previn, who came to the London Symphony Orchestra from America, has now taken to London as his adopted city. He is a very attractive personality, seemingly unspoilt by the huge and varied musical successes in his relatively short life (he was born in 1934). He is absorbed by everything to do with his job as principal conductor of the LSO, by the people in and about it. Part of his success lies, no doubt, in his native curiosity over all things that make up life, and the ingenuous delight which he experiences and radiates when he discovers a 'new' composer or composition, new to himself. To possess such a modesty is rare in one who may well claim to live on the edge of genius, a word that must always be used sparingly and with the utmost discretion.

And still in London—Colin Davis. Nobody is yet absolutely certain what to make of this gentleman. He swam into the top flight of conductors when he took over a concert performance of *Don Giovanni* at a moment's notice from the indisposed Otto Klemperer in 1959. Since then he has been, in too quick succession for comfort, Musical Director of Sadler's Wells Opera; conductor of the BBC Symphony Orchestra and also conductor of the Last Night of the Proms; and Musical Director at Covent Garden. Still in his forties he has almost reached the peak in England, musically speaking. Where is there left for him to go in a conducting capacity? And the fact that he never stays long anywhere must indicate itchy feet, if nothing else.

All these brilliant people prefer the moderate line with composers' works, and while you might think this smacks of the humdrum, it most certainly does not. It is far more difficult and requires patience and understanding to keep things going in a restrained manner, than to give way to sudden excesses for the sake of an effect, which is still the way with some inexperienced, 'twilight' conductors, but no longer with the older ones. There is just one of them left, one of the old generation, an old wizard who seems ancient when you see him in his dressing room or clambering into his car after the concert. I am referring to Leopold Stokowski, or 'Stokey' as musicians call him on account of the fact that he was born in London in 1882 and christened (or baptised, I suppose) with the English name of Stokes, a corruption of his Polish parents' surname to which he reverted for professional reasons, even attaching a central European accent to his new image. Well, that image is not new by any means, nor is it tarnished. There are purists who object to the fact that he is given to monkeying about with the score, but this is to achieve a pronounced effect which, in the 1930s, when Stokey was most active, was necessary to combat the rising and over-dramatic influence of the cinema. And it was with Disney's film *Fantasia* that he made a great name for himself on the screen, popularising (in the nicest sense) works by mainly Bach, Stravinsky and Beethoven. Stokey also appeared in a film about a destitute orchestra called *A Hundred Men and a Girl* which was also a vehicle for the young Canadian singing-child-actress Deanna Durbin. Watching this film again recently (it must have been made in 1934) and comparing Stokey's action then, and now when he last came here, it has not altered at all. He still uses no baton and manages to get amazing results by sheer dynamism and a powerful, self-originated conducting technique. His *Sixth Symphony* of Tchaikovsky was an outstanding performance. Stokey is a great joker, and if you do not see through his comic turn of mind you will never get close to him, for his attitude is very much that of the grand seigneur. And when he is in London, he will probably trot off, by car now, to St John's Wood to 'look for his old nurse'.

Another conductor who was not averse to changing the score of dead, but never of living composers, was Sir Thomas Beecham. It was always done very carefully, even affectionately, full of intrinsic feeling and merit and never to caricature the music or its original intentions. His arrangements include Handel's music for *The Gods go a' Begging* (a ballet score); *The Great Elopement* (an orchestral suite); his re-orchestration (or *realisation* as such deeds are often politely called) of Grétry's *Zémire et Azor* and many voluptuous presentations of minor French pieces, often served up as encores and described by Beecham himself as 'lollipops'. This is the best kind of arranging, although whether it was the intrinsic material which came through or the magic which Beecham had wrought on it, nobody could tell. Since his day the practice of 'lollipops' has unfortunately disappeared, and it was such a good way of widening the listener's awareness to some of the byways of music.

It is often galling to musicians to hear the glorification that accompanies a famous conductor to his grave, when everybody closely connected with him knew full well that he had been exceedingly unpleasant. But because he had been pig-rude, overbearing, impatient, vain, intolerant, a bully and lacking in all consideration for others, he got results, and by his results the public knew and worshipped him. At the end of the performance the players, who had suffered the worst, knew that they had contributed to a great performance, were never at a loss to know what to do during it, and at the local at closing time were bound to agree with one another that they all felt completely satisfied with their evening's work. It is not often that this can happen, but when it does the conductor and the players have managed to bring off a superior performance. This is not to say that every time a Prom audience goes mad with enthusiasm, the magic has been wrought in the same way. It is very easy to give the effect of a good performance, and when the audience is utterly receptive this goes even further to create an illusion of artistic success. It may even fool our music critics but the musicians know all right, they know the corners that have been cut, the *rubato* so out of place but so effective, in a cheap sort of way, that it got sighs of ecstasy.

The best conductor is born and not made. Passable conductors are born and then work like slaves to make themselves even better. They possess in their cradles what is required, and what other aspirants, no matter how hard, how devotedly they try, can never attain. Many a well-trained, innately musical, thoroughly intelligent, industrious and endearing person founders before he has established himself. A little spark is missing; by comparison with all the other accomplishments it may be a tiny part, but it is all important. It can be a number of things, but one of them undoubtedly has got to be ruthlessness, cruelty, beastliness, call it what you will. For a good conductor, in order to achieve what he *knows* is right, to get what he must have for the performance, has got to be able to regard his own technique as read, so that he can devote all his thoughts to the shaping of the rehearsals and the wise allocation of time to the most awkward passages or movements. One conductor who came into the class of the great ones, sometimes found that his technique did let him down, although he would be the last person to admit it. And that was Beecham. Even so, he was held in the greatest respect and, in a way, a curious affection by his players. It was more than an experience to play for him: it was generally an uproarious education. Yet there were times when, in the course of a work, one would see him look down at the score, and the right hand began to go round in circles over his head like a distress signal. This is exactly what it was, an indication that he had lost himself. But the players always sailed on and brought him safely to port. The great feeling and delicacy that Beecham was able to bring to the works he conducted has never been matched. He always turned out a concert that was interesting, exciting, special and, above all, sounded authentic. This was providing he had not had a programme forced on him. When that happened, which was rarely, the result never sounded authentic. A performance of Beethoven's 'Choral' Symphony at an Edinburgh Festival was far from authentic, and only displayed how ill at ease Beecham was with the whole idea. He never liked to conduct any work for which he had not complete personal sympathy and fondness; and even though his choice might sometimes seem questionable, he was still able to invest even the most trivial compositions with such sparkle and vivacity as to elevate them to masterpieces.

Malcolm Sargent, despite his great reputation and mystique which he wove round himself, and despite the most heroic last few years of his life which nobody would wish to belittle, was not one of England's greatest conductors. He had patches of woolliness, of indecision and of sheer forgetfulness that only his personality and his always immaculate appearance were able to salve. All the same he was very generously disposed to musicians and had a very wide following, partly on account of his noble handling of the Promenade Concerts. At one time he had hoped to start a new career by taking up an old one again. Once upon a time he had been conductor of the D'Oyly Carte Opera for many years and, until their copyright ran out, the only professional company allowed to perform the operas of Gilbert and Sullivan.

In 1954 he was engaged to conduct Sir William Walton's opera *Troilus and Cressida* at Covent Garden, a truly all-British affair. Not only did Sargent do a less than first class job, but he also fell foul of the general administrator of the day, David Webster. Webster told him that there was no job for him there because he did not support their cause at the Royal Opera House: the cause of homosexuality.

Sargent was a great social butterfly, and moth. There is a completely untrue story that is cruel, but all too characteristic about him at the Victory Parade in 1946, walking down the Mall towards Buckingham Palace together with Winston Churchill, the hero of the hour (and of the decade). The then King and Queen were on the balcony, acknowledging the cheers of the crowd, when suddenly the Queen turned to the King and asked: 'Bertie, tell me, who is that large man with a cigar walking next to Malcolm?'

We are not without our charlatans today, masquerading as conductors. They lack the three basic qualities which are essential: self-confidence, the ability to inspire confidence in others, and the facility for getting exactly what they want from even the most uncooperative players. One peripatetic European lacks all these. He used to be a very good instrumentalist but, it is said, once declared: 'I have suffered so much in the past from bad conductors, that I shall become one myself and torture other musicians.' It is not entirely clear whether he meant that he intended to become merely a conductor or a bad conductor like those he was criticising, but he has very definitely managed to be thoroughly bad.

This man gets up on the box for the rehearsals, and with scarcely the hint of welcome in his face at the first one, and a mere apology for a handshake to the leader (who is a first-class musician), begins with the vaguest gesture of a beat, leaning back against the rail in an attitude of boredom. After only a few bars he stops the orchestra. They are not sure why, because his grasp of our language is insecure and fractured. So they start again. And stop again. And so it goes on until this conductor forces someone in the orchestra to complain. An argument ensues, he utters highly treasonable expressions about the English, and walks out. After cajolement and soft soap he agrees to return, and somehow, but in an atmosphere that is positively freezing, he manages to get through the programme. At the end of the rehearsal he walks out, saying nothing, thanking nobody.

But at the concert it is a different matter altogether. All is smiles. The great conductor is before his audience. They love him, he loves them, he loves the orchestra—or so it appears. But the orchestra still doesn't love him a bit, especially as he has again varied the special instructions and markings made, altered, cancelled and modified at rehearsal. Now he suddenly does something entirely different and without warning, so that the leader is permanently on the edge of his seat, making instant decisions, often against the conductor's indications, such as they are. The whole orchestra have one eye on him, and if possible a glance at this conductor who is battering his way through the works which they all know so well. The rehearsals have all been for the conductor, whose vague arm movements impress nobody.

After the concert with champagne and a few invited guests, not one from the orchestra, this conductor changes his personality to the very centre of good fun and amusing anecdotes, to humour and an inexhaustible fund of stories. He is entirely different, but he has got to be in the centre of things all the same. This is how he relaxes after, he will say, a very difficult time with the orchestra. But the whole difficulty for him is that he is scared stiff of them, in case anyone should show him up, because he knows quite well that he cannot conduct. Hence the play at not being able to speak good English, but even that is a defence.

Why do some conductors behave so badly? What seems to give them the right to vent their feelings in exactly the way we would all like to be able to do at one time or another? How do they get away with it when we wouldn't? The answer must surely be that they are rather special people. The kind of lives they lead by virtue of the dictates of their job means that they cannot be classified as 'normal' in the sense that a civil servant or a doctor or a bus driver is so considered. For a conductor—or indeed for any musician and actor—there is not the same routine in his daily round, not the same work-pattern which leaves him free every evening and at the weekend. A conductor is part of that glamorous occupation called show-business, whose participants work to give the rest of the world, the 'normal' ones, their recreation. Consequently the conductor, above all, is owed a little latitude, some extra perks for the enormous pleasure which he is able to give to thousands of people, pleasure and excitement too, in their often drab, grey lives.

Toscanini, as we have discovered, was one of the rudest conductors in living memory, and no one in Britain would be prepared to put up with that sort of treatment today, the day of the Union. And in certain respects, I cannot but have sympathy for the musician. Nor would George Szell be so easily tolerated either, in his worst moods. He could fly into the most terrible rages that had to be seen to be believed, because of the suddenness with which they came and went. I attended rehearsals of Szell's from time to time, and those with his own orchestra, the Cleveland Orchestra, were fraught with a tense atmosphere. It was so tense that the impression was of everybody being on edge, cowed, slightly brow-beaten. One wonders whether this is the best way to get the best out of people. Yet Szell, with his huge eyes, magnified by enormous spectacles, his bald head, almost hairless face and large lips, was a kind and very likeable man off the box. He had a searing mind that cut straight through to the topic under discussion, never wavering, never spending a moment on anything trivial. A strange person, and a very brilliant one.

It is likely that many conductors behave differently when they are on the box from when they are off it, and that this fact escapes them. Whether they assume a delusion of real power when they step up those few inches, whether it is all a demonstration of insecurity which makes them become, or try to become conductors, varies from one to another.

So the players sometimes try to find out by indulging in the hoary old sport of conductor-baiting. It takes various forms and the more the subject rises to the bait, the more chance there is of the occupation being continued. Anybody who has ever been in authority knows that the best way to stop real trouble is to nip this sort of nonsense in the bud. A conductor's authority is a variable thing and will depend a good deal upon the circumstances in which he finds himself.

If he is working with one of the independent orchestras and trouble starts, the board of directors of the orchestra, all playing members, will be present and will instantly take action themselves. Either they agree with the complaint and talk to the conductor privately, or else they support him at once and quell the disturbance with their own authority. In any of the BBC orchestras there will be the leader who may very well call for order and get it; there is always the producer in attendance, who is officially in charge of proceedings from the time the rehearsal starts to the end of the recording; and there is the orchestral manager. Between them they can usually ensure that the session continues, so as not to waste time, and deal with the matter afterwards, or in the break, if it needs discussion or a written report made. Generally speaking, and unless the circumstances are very unusual, the line will be to support the conductor.

Artistically the conductor is always in charge. He has to make all the musical decisions, and it is because of his character and personality, his experience and his reputation that such events should never happen. If it does, he will deal with the trouble instantly and firmly, though pleasantly and will, if he can find one that is apt, finish with a joke, providing it is not completely at the expense of his adversary of the moment.

Putting a young conductor 'up in front' of a seasoned bunch of professional musicians is rather like casting him to the lions if he tries to be unduly assertive or puts up their backs by being cocky. An elderly and highly respected percussion player, now retired, once objected to being asked to play a passage in a Beethoven symphony in what he considered an unusual manner. 'Klemperer and Karajan have it the way I played it [note the order of priorities!] so why do you want it different?' he asked. The young conductor insisted that this was how he wanted it and asked his senior in age by about twice, to conform. 'Well all right, I'll play it your way now, but it'll be done my way at the performance,' came the grudging reply. Of course the conductor never dreamed that he meant it, so that when it came out 'Klemperer's and Karajan's and his' way before the audience, the conductor's face was a study.

Possibly the most destructive gambit that malicious players can devise to tease an inexperienced or a weak conductor, is to stop the rehearsal proceeding by means of a variety of ostensibly reasonable interruptions. They may complain of discomfort through their desks being too close together and then, when they are moved, they will be too far apart, but other desks will, by then, have been affected too. Or the lighting may be inadequate, or too bright, with beams shining into players' faces. Or it may be too hot, or too cold or too draughty or too stuffy; or somebody may not be able to see the conductor properly (a ripe one, this). Then two or three players will ask the conductor questions relating to their printed parts, even going up to him with the music, perhaps banging into other players' stands and sending their music flying. It is all too easy for the complete rehearsal to be broken up within a few moments. Other players, not immediately involved, will be enjoying the charade immensely, and unless the leader is the first to call a halt it will become irretrievable. It can happen, and even to those on the side of authority, it is not without its humour.

On rare occasions, however, everybody unites to act against the conductor's wishes, management included. I remember such an occasion on a Sunday in Edinburgh, when the conductor objected to a wind machine that was being used at the morning rehearsal. He insisted that another one be found, one less disreputable, and in better working order, in fact a new one. Anybody who has been in Edinburgh on a Sunday knows what chance there is of being able to buy a pin, let alone a wind machine. The BBC were tried in Glasgow. Had they a wind machine? The man on the news desk took it for a piece of rudery and was about to ring off, but when the question was explained and somebody telephoned to find out, a parallel call was already being put through to the Scottish National Orchestra. Both drew a blank. The percussion player in charge of the section was, understandably, getting a little anxious, and so we hit on a plan. He would go down to Leith and buy a piece of sail-cloth. No doubt they would help him to get it stitched on to the wind machine tightly and looking fresh. Meanwhile a few small bits of wood to repair those broken slats and a dab of quick-drying paint here and there. The object looked a good deal more respectable at the performance in spite of the fact that not all the slats had been repaired, and the conductor never said anything about it!

There's a good game that is worth playing when there is a real old orchestral veteran about, and in a mood to demonstrate how many celebrated conductors he has played under. It starts quite casually, in a bar, like this:

'What did you think of W?'

'Him?'—in disbelief that anyone would want to ask. 'A useless one he was. Nasty too. Used to pick on a player and never leave him alone all through rehearsals—if you could call them that.'

'I see, well how about Y, then?' one pursues. There is a swallow of rage.

'He's useless'.

'And what about X? Did you ever work with him?'

'Yes, he's all right. Bit of a berk. Can't conduct anyway.'

By now the audience will have grown, and other people will be throwing in names and warming to the game.

'What can you tell us of Z?' someone else asks. And the fount of all orchestral wisdom is enjoying himself enormously as well.

'Don't talk to me about him. Here, get me another pint of this. Biggest berk of all. Couldn't conduct to save his life. Went on telling stories that nobody understood. He waved his arms about. If there were twenty-four beats to the bar we got every one. Never knew where you were. Good for a pint though.'

And so it goes on, through the list of conductors. When the big ones have been exhausted, he goes on to the small ones. It's a good game, but of course it is a terrible lot of rubbish, because the only criterion players have of a 'good' conductor is one who finishes rehearsing early and lets them all do what they want.

7

MANAGEMENT

THE VERY FIRST KIND OF ORCHESTRA BELONGED TO AN
archduke and, as we well know, Mozart, Haydn and Beethoven each depended on the munificence of princelings and pre-
lates, while Bach was solely supported by the Church and wrote
the majority of his compositions as part of his job. The German
States (or Kingdoms as they were) and the Austro-Hungarian
Empire was advanced in thought over the matter of orchestras
supported by the exchequer, and they continued to be through
two wars and up to the present day. Only the Berlin Philharmonic Orchestra had some independence, which was threatened
during the Nazi régime until it was taken over by Hitler and the
State to save it from financial disaster.

In Britain there are no orchestras that are state supported
outside the BBC, although the independent ones are approach-
ing this situation in London via a co-ordinating body called the
London Orchestral Concerts Board. In the provinces the local
councils support their orchestras via the rates, but do not insist
upon complete control.

Sir Thomas Beecham was the last autocratic owner of an
orchestra, and before him Walter Legge could claim to possess
the only other one in London that did what he said. With
Beecham it had been the Beecham Orchestra, the London Philharmonic Orchestra (LPO) and lastly the Royal Philharmonic
Orchestra (RPO). He not only paid all the orchestras' deficits
but had a complete say in their policies and programmes. Walter
Legge, a shrewd musician and businessman from what is now
EMI Records, founded the Philharmonia Orchestra in 1945
especially to make gramophone records. They were good, the
orchestra being recruited from among the very best musicians in
London, so much so that it attracted the finest conductors from a
Europe that was getting back on to its feet again. von Karajan,
Toscanini, Cantelli, Klemperer and many others then unknown

made their post war conducting débuts with the Philharmonia.

In the case of Legge, ill-health and sheer strain caused him to leave England, and death took Sir Thomas. The two orchestras were left high and dry, unsupported by their former, wealthy owners, and threatened with extinction. This did not happen to the orchestras simultaneously, but to the Philharmonia first. Its members got together and decided that they would form themselves into a limited company, which they did. They secured the advice and some financial backing from musically minded merchants, and have since carried on as the New Philharmonia Orchestra (NPO). When Beecham died the Royal Philharmonic Orchestra looked as if it might go under. A newspaper campaign that began with letters to *The Times* whipped up support, mainly from people who had never even been to its concerts. But it survived and has had until the end of 1974 as its chief conductor Rudolf Kempe, whom Beecham appointed with almost his dying breath.

The other two main London orchestras, the London Symphony Orchestra (LSO) and the London Philharmonic Orchestra (LPO) have been self-governing bodies since 1904 and 1939 respectively, and what more or less happened was that the two orchestras mentioned above fell into line with them. Even so, it was a most unusual situation for an orchestra to be self-governing as early as 1904.

The London Orchestral Concerts Board (LOCB) mentioned briefly above, is a name that is not to be found in reference books. It administers the four main London orchestras (the LSO, the LPO, the RPO and the NPO), arranges sensible and non-conflicting programmes in the London area, and gives subsidies. Each one of these orchestras has now got one substantial industrial backer: Peter Stuyvesant for the LSO, W.D & H.O. Wills for the LPO and so on. They also have other backers who are trustees of the orchestra and sit on the trustees' board, but not on the board which actually controls the orchestra's life. But this is not sufficient to keep them going financially, and the four orchestras look to what is virtually a state subsidy to help them even further in this vastly expensive business of running an orchestra.

The LOCB has funds drawn in equal proportions from the Arts Council and the Greater London Council, and makes a grant to each orchestra according to the number of concerts it gives at the Royal Festival Hall and at the Fairfield Halls, Croydon, but *not* the Royal Albert Hall. This privately owned building is considered to be in competition with the Royal Festival Hall, and so will be the City of London's new Barbican Concert Hall when it is eventually finished. With this form of control, the LOCB insist upon monitoring the programmes which the four London orchestras present at the Festival Hall. The BBC are also involved in this to a lesser extent, as the BBC Symphony Orchestra plays there on one Wednesday a month. The same work is not permitted to be heard (unless for a very special reason) within eight weeks. It was lightheartedly suggested before the Beethoven bicentenary that he be commemorated by having *none* of his works performed! Since they form the staple diet of many concerts, Beethoven's works are to be heard all the year round. His bicentenary meant that a number of seldom-played works were dragged out only to be revealed as best left in limbo for the next hundred years.

The LOCB places no restrictions upon the orchestras save in 'clashes' of works, and in the sheer number of concert dates available to them. The board consists of the Director and the Associate Director of the Royal Festival Hall, their planning manager and one or sometimes two representatives from the Arts Council. But as ordinary meetings are over programmes and allocation of dates, it is a planning matter and dealt with at the RFH where these meetings take place.

Programme planning itself is done within each of the four orchestras by the board and the general manager in association with the various conductors who are involved in the season's concerts. This often means trans-Atlantic telephone calls and telegrams because the best conductors are always flying about from place to place and are difficult to catch by ordinary post. And these four orchestras do succeed in giving us the best of the world's conductors and soloists.

The policy of these orchestras is dealt with again by the respective boards. This is elected annually from the whole orchestra, and from among those players who get the (usually) five most votes. The five men so constituted as the board elect their chairman from their own knowledge of the resources which they all possess. He has a grant of a small amount for special travel and entertaining expenses, but the remainder do their work without payment. It often involves a great deal of spare time being given for the benefit of the orchestra, and only those who are this way inclined, or who see their usefulness to the orchestra soon coming to an end, musically speaking, wish to involve themselves in this manner. Yet without any business training at all and often without very much knowledge of the world and its ways, these men conduct the running and the future of a great orchestra in their spare time, sometimes well, sometimes disastrously. It is really a question of how the outside forces come into play upon them.

The LPO apart, each of the other three orchestras employs a full-time general manager to run the office and to carry out the policy of the orchestra as it is shaped by the board, usually with him in attendance. In the LSO, the RPO and the NPO, this general manager is a servant of the orchestra, he can be overruled and is not a member of the board, which places him in a most invidious position. The ideal situation exists in the LPO, where the general manager, called the managing director, is a full member of the board and his vote carries equally with the others. Since he had formerly been a trumpet player in the LPO and found himself well able to care for the orchestra's affairs, he stayed on the board and became the principal executive of the orchestra as well. This man, Eric Bravington, richly deserves the CBE which he was awarded in January 1973. In his position of real authority he can cut through some of the absurd and naïve suggestions which come from the usual board members, and get things done.

Not so, the other general managers. They sometimes find themselves hamstrung by ill-advised demands counter to what they, who regard themselves as businessmen, consider to be right in the circumstances. But these three orchestras have suffered in their own ways and want to control their own destinies. Beecham and Legge in the RPO and Philharmonia respectively often whirled the orchestra about in a manner which was found distasteful. Others in the LSO have overstepped the bounds of their jobs and, in referring to 'my orchestra' (which it is all too easy to do) have upset their employers, the players. But it does require one person in command, one person who can be sure of being able to carry out a sensible policy without inter-

ruption or a watering down of its course. The trouble is that we
are all mortal, and one man with all this authority can soon turn
into a tyrant. This is what the orchestras are afraid of, and this
is what the union does not want either; they want only an
orchestra composed of union members run by themselves. All
the same it is interesting to note the change in outlook of
orchestral members against the union, once they become
directors.

The general manager is usually engaged by a management
consultant organisation, which is about the worst possible concern to choose such a person, just in the same way as it is
virtually useless when 'going-over' an orchestra to suggest im-
provements and savings in its running. I once had a meeting
with one of these no doubt efficient business men and he proceeded to inform me that a situation depended upon whether
Beethoven's Sixth or 'Pastoral' symphony was being played.
He hadn't even done his homework.

Once appointed, the general manager will undoubtedly
attempt to carve his way through the office in the shortest
possible time so as to get to the many dozen outstanding and
vitally urgent matters by now overdue. From then on it means
burning the midnight oil, carrying round a hand-dictating
machine to use at every available opportunity. And there will
always be those time-wasters, either on the telephone or in
person. The answer is a good telephone and front-door protec-
tive system to discourage having one's privacy invaded. Staff
in an orchestral office is really no problem because of the great
attraction which the job possesses, but the immediately supporting troops of accountant, programme planner and switch-
board operator must all be of prime calibre. The post of orchestral
manager is a very highly paid job and it really suits only a
handful of men. The salary may sound good, but like a doctor,
one never knows whether the telephone is going to go in the
night with the need to awake, think, and decide at some un-
godly hour. I know more people who have turned down the
offer of general manager of one of the four London orchestras
than have accepted it. But it has its enormous compensations,
like prestige, and being in the swim of the world's musical life,
if you want that.

The BBC is utterly different. There are about 25,000

employees in this organisation, and sometimes, when one wants a quick decision, it appears that every one of them is being consulted. There are twelve orchestras in the Corporation. The BBC Symphony Orchestra, the Concert Orchestra, the Radio Orchestra and the London Studio Players are all based in London. Of them, only the Symphony Orchestra comes under the control of the Music Division, the others are under the network called Radio 1 and 2. This is particularly odd in the case of the Concert Orchestra, whose most useful work is done for Radio 3, and whose sole claims to connections with Radio 2 are in a programme called *Melodies for You* (which frankly could just as well be done on records), and the fast-declining though once classic of its kind, *Friday Night is Music Night*.

Outside London there are three BBC regional symphony orchestras: the Northern, the Scottish and the Welsh, of which the latter is grossly under-strung. Besides these, there is the BBC Midland Radio Orchestra, the Northern Dance Orchestra, the New Scottish Radio Orchestra and the Northern Ireland Orchestra, also 'light'.

In addition, and rather behind the cow's tail, is the former New BBC Orchestra, changed by order of the Musicians' Union to the BBC Training Orchestra, and now called, somewhat pompously 'The Academy of the BBC'. Since it is being run down and will soon disappear, I put it at the end. It is designed to give music students two or three years of playing in an orchestra, and is unique in Great Britain. Its usefulness cannot be over-emphasised because it has turned out a number of excellent players who, unlike many of their contemporaries from the London schools of music, are absolutely at home in orchestras, sometimes in positions of responsibility, which only sitting and playing in orchestras can give. The Academy recruits other players locally to its centre in Bristol, and plays the symphonic repertoire.

The management of these orchestras falls into three distinct formats. The BBC Symphony Orchestra has a general manager *and* a manager, at present both men. The Concert Orchestra has a male manager and a male assistant who also devotes some of his time especially to the London Studio Players (commonly known as 'The Unit'). The Radio Orchestra has a male manager. All the other orchestras have women 'orchestral

(above) *Rehearsal for a broadcast by the BBC Symphony Orchestra under Pierre Boulez in their No. 1 studio at Maida Vale;* (below) *a concert at the Royal Festival Hall, London*

Promenade Concert at the Royal Albert Hall, London. One of the Last Nights under Sir Malcolm Sargent

assistants', but in every case they are responsible to a man who is a music producer in the region, or else head of music there.

This structure differs radically from independent orchestras. There the musicians are far too independent to need looking after very much, and the nearest person to them on the management side is the personnel manager, who is really the 'fixer' (see p. 116). But he is not the one to go to with complaints of a general nature, better one of the board, who is on the spot, and if necessary via him to the general manager in the office.

There is an old concept in commerce that 'The job of a manager is to manage'. In the BBC, which is after all a commercial enterprise these days, it is not necessarily the case at all. Four out of the five male orchestral managers in London have little authority of their own. They know the troublesome players and keep them down as best they can, but they cannot get rid of them simply because they have a nuisance value. The outside orchestras can and do. In any case, provided that the playing of BBC musicians is acceptable, the resident conductor will probably side with them, because it is their playing which concerns him most. And that is reasonable enough. All the manager can do is to reduce rising temperatures by soft words, by calling meetings and explaining what he is doing, and generally by fussing round like an old hen with errant chicks. Unless a manager is given 'teeth', that is to say, the full authority and power to bite back if he is bitten, he will earn little respect, and may even get by-passed when complaints are flying and the orchestra is upset. Back to the power of the union again, which is far greater than any one manager's, and the union does not deal with anybody of such lowly status in any case. So he must keep the equilibrium as level as possible, be adroit, and at all times keep a cool head. It is a very thankless job, during which he must never for one moment imagine that he has a single friend among the players.

The manager must never at any time appear to be refusing the players anything; never be too busy to answer the most piffling question; never too pressed to listen to a rambling story about the holidays or the passionate events of the past evening, or the impossible demands of the wife; never disinterested or unamused by some dreadful and vulgar story, first heard at school and now trotted out as new. The manager must, in other words, always be as pleasant and absorbent as the local vicar, but without that worthy's obligation to make additions to his flock.

The manager must also possess that rare faculty of knowing when to be at the right place at the right time. The right place is not hard to divine, for that is where the orchestra is playing or rehearsing; but it is the right time that matters just as much. Not only has he to be there when anything is wrong, but if possible before that happens. Thus he needs second sight, so as to be able to show himself, waiting for the event or events to take place.

The manager must not be so stand-offiish as to refuse to have a drink sometimes with the musicians. But he should try not to meet the same ones over and over again or otherwise rumours and jealousies will develop among the others, especially among those who do not drink at all. He must live on a slightly different plane from the musicians, only occasionally, and then if possible in unfamiliar surroundings, meeting them on theirs. But never in his own surroundings.

Yet when one of the players is in real trouble, actual or only imagined, he will invariably find that his manager, whom he has treated with disdain and even enmity, is sympathetic and helpful and will be prepared to talk about it and to try and put things right. Ill-health and women are the usual reasons; or ill-health and men in the case of women players.

There is now only one all-male orchestra in Britain, the London Symphony Orchestra. All male, that is to say, except for the occasional lady harpist when Osian Ellis is not with them. This does make life easy, because there has only to be one woman as a member of an orchestra for the whole atmosphere to change. Orchestral men behave so much better when there are no women about, and whether they know it or not, women are the root cause of many of the upsets in mixed orchestras. Sex raises its ugly head in a number of different ways, sometimes obviously, at other times slyly. Certain trouble-makers may not even realise that what they are doing is to impress others, and women in particular, even though the subconscious objects of their endeavours remain for ever oblivious, like those characters in a Chekov play who never appreciate what is going on all round them.

On the other hand, liaisons and multiple liaisons go on all the

time among the players, but with never a punch-up to crown a
jealous scene. I once sat looking at an orchestra, pondering on
whom I could really count on to back me up in a fight. The most
I felt I could optimistically expect was half of one man, according
to how much drink he had had. The reason for this is that musicians depend either on their hands if they are string or percussion
players, or on their mouths and hands if they are wind players.
Somebody else's fist in the mouth of a clarinettist might easily
put paid to his career for ever. A broken finger on the left hand
of a violinist would prevent his working for weeks. Musicians
do not want to be involved in any physical violence, that is why
they are such experts at mental violence. But it does seem odd
that the worst kind of jealous scene between two men over one
woman in an orchestra can end without blows being struck,
merely foul words and threats.

There can be no question whatever of the manager of an
orchestra striking up a friendship with somebody of the opposite
sex in that orchestra (or of the same sex for that matter should
he be a homosexual, and I have not met one of those yet).
There is nothing surer than this to deprive him of the last vestige
of authority and set the whole pack of orchestral wolves howling
at his heels. And the poor woman will be no better off either.
Nobody will be able to voice their thoughts in public in case they
get back 'to the office'. This is the sure way of managerial
suicide, for there can be no secrets in an orchestra, least of all
such a one as this.

Possibly the most difficult aspect of being an orchestral manager is to be able to regard not only the people, but also the job
entirely compassionately and coldly. It comes in the end, after
disillusionment and disappointment. It is altogether as exhausting as it can be pleasant. The best part of it is that he is able to
hear live music played whenever he likes, if indeed he likes
music, and if what his orchestra plays is also the sort of music he
would listen to for preference. This does not necessarily follow.
And if he is not listening to the orchestra and is in his office,
attending to the hundred and one things vital to the orchestra's
administration, he is doing the one part of the job which the
players never understand. 'Why do you spend so much time in
the office?' they ask. 'Whatever do you *do* there?' This is a
question which cannot be answered in brief. 'You don't have to

work out the pay,' they go on; 'you aren't taking us out anywhere this week, so why are you in the office? Have you got a
new secretary you keep there whom we don't know about? And
what happened to that one with the big eyes?' Such questions
are probably best left unanswered, or half-answered by way of an
excuse to bring the silly monologue to an end. The administration of an orchestra's players, especially within the BBC, is a
taxing business, taxing on time and on health. Nervous ex-
haustion is a common ailment among orchestral managers,
wherever they work, and especially if they take their job to heart.

FIXERS

The booking of players is done by someone known throughout
the profession as a 'fixer'. Every orchestra has its own fixer and
he has a large and valuable list of players for all imaginable
instruments, with their addresses and, more important, their
telephone numbers. He will know which are most reliable, which
are most liked by their colleagues, and which, in the case of real
specialists, are the ones to go for in any particular work. Naturally most of these lists overlap, but they arc the absolute musical
bibles for each orchestra when it comes to needing extra players
and deputy players at short notice, like our friend in the preface
to this book. There is a good deal of exchange between orchestral
fixers too, regarding people whose habits have changed, who
have spectacularly declined in performance. They will be more
chary of passing on news of a player whose performance is
improving, for he will be regarded as a 'find' and will be given a
lot of work. The really important fixers, in financial terms, are
those who look after the film studios, the television shows and the
recording companies, when these do not use a permanent orchestra. Three of the most successful fixers in this line are
instrumentalists themselves, and play on all the sessions which
they fix. Thereby they collect their own fee, 50p per player whom
they have selected for the session, a great deal of prestige, goodwill, fear and hatred, taken all round. They are all Jewish, but
this does not prevent them from receiving many useful and
desirable presents from their faithful followers at Christmas.
   The Jewish element in music is too strong to be overlooked.

They are quite often very talented musicians, and in some cases spectacularly so. Furthermore it is mainly Jewish businessmen who sponsor much of London's and Manchester's and Glasgow's music, and who eventually get their knighthoods for service to music. Well deserved too, for without this Jewish backing in Britain, it is very doubtful whether the musical scene, as we know it, could possibly continue. This was brought very much to mind when a Christian Lord Mayor of London started a fund for Cathedral Choirs. It was a disastrous failure because no Jew would wish to contribute towards Christian foundations, however obliquely.

A great number of ordinary musicians are Jewish, in any case, and hail from that part of London known as British West Hampstead. The one day of the year on which *not* to give a concert, and expect to find deputies at short notice, is the Jewish Day of Atonement; when, of course, and for the same reason, it is unlikely that you will be able to get hold of a London taxi either.

AUDITIONS

Although management recruits extras and deputies through fixers, the more permanent vacancies are filled by the established practice of auditions. The procedure varies, but the principle is one of active competition against other contestants—one at a time of course. In considering a rank and file vacancy, and the business of finding the right player to fill it, there are a number of differences which crop up on both sides of the audition table, if it is a properly organised affair.

The Berlin Philharmonic Orchestra is the most daunting, and at the same time the most democratic. Every member of the orchestra is present, and while few of them say what they think, applause is certainly the order of the day if they like the player. But it must be a fearsome experience to play for the best orchestra in the world under such circumstances and with a hundred pairs of eyes and ears focused upon you.

Other independent orchestras usually get a player in and give him a trial run for a while, but they may hear him first, just a few of them, quietly after a session. It's all very circumspect, if not secretive. And if they don't like his playing or his personality they say no more and never book him again. Unless he is a numskull he will understand and not pester them for a decision.

The BBC likes to be scrupulously fair about it all and fall over themselves to appear so by having auditions that are set-piece affairs. The orchestra's conductor, leader, orchestral manager and principal of the section sit round a table and are joined by a musician who is a known master of the instrument to be heard, and who is nothing to do with the BBC. This 'outside assessor' is therefore neutral and has no preconceived notions about the post to be filled. Sometimes, and more often than not, he has his own pupils, which is why he may look down the list of entrants and say 'No. 3 and No. 7 are going to recognise me. I hope they don't let me down, but obviously I'm biased in their cases so you won't expect me to write a report, will you?' This is agreed because it is unusual for no single pupil of the assessor (whether past or present) to turn up, especially if they have heard it is he who is on the panel.

The outside assessor can or need not enter too forcibly into the proceedings. One of the best pieces of one-upmanship that I ever saw in musical circles related to the assessor and the prepared piece which every candidate is asked to bring along and play. It is entirely of his own choosing, and the choice often gives a guide to the person. On this occasion the chosen piece involved a turn of the page part of the way through. Without warning, this assessor got up, walked over to the music stand and without looking or being able to see the part, turned the page at exactly the right moment for the player. He was so familiar with the work, and its edition, that he had it engraved on his memory. Since it was a work that had gone into many and varied editions, the impressive performance was that of the assessor, not the player.

Some candidates come along with the most ridiculous of prepared pieces, and almost disqualify themselves before they start to play, because of the inappropriate nature of the work. The best way to go about it is to err on the side of simplicity and play the thing properly, not flounder through some *avant-garde* stuff in the hope that nobody will know it well enough to tell which are the wrong notes. The conductor, the leader and above all the assessor take a lot of fooling. Some candidates talk all the way through the ordeal so as to cover their own nervous condition and their deficiencies; there are those who argue; there are those who complain; there are those who act the idiot and pretend it just isn't their day.

The wise ones choose a fairly short, not too difficult piece, which enables the player to show variety of tempo and mood. If he plays it nicely, he is on the way to receiving the panel's approval for the next, harder step. This is the sight-reading. Normally pieces are chosen which not only reflect the orchestra's usual type of musical fare, but which are not too difficult either. It is no good tying a player in knots so that he cannot show his capabilities, when this is the only reason for his attending the audition. If he is to sit near the front of the section, he will be expected to know the conventional works for the instrument, even from memory. If a cellist, and due to sit at the front or the second desk, he must know the cello quartet from the Overture to *William Tell*. If he offers to play these hardy perennials from memory and can do so, that is a bonus. But if he boasts that he can and then makes a hash of them, nobody is interested in him.

Almost everybody who attends an audition is nervous, and the panel not only expect but look for this. A player who displays no nerves at all may be so insensitive that he is not suitable to join the orchestra. But even so, the right sort of technique overrides bad nerves and allows the player to give a good showing once he has settled down.

It is not too easy for the panel to remain totally absorbed in each candidate after hours of hearing a string of mainly indifferent players. Neither will they tend to remain totally serious-minded or sometimes be able, except with the utmost difficulty, to preserve a neutral and impassive expression on their faces. The members of this august and mightily feared group of perfectly harmless and rather pleasant people may be observed passing notes to one another. These will not always read 'Very curious fingering: doesn't seem to appreciate what note is on the adjoining string', but rather 'If the blighter doesn't stop twitching, I shall have to go out'.

But the panel is serious all the same, and are out to find the best person or persons for the job, both as player and as regards personality. Who knows, whether one may be recommending an impossible eccentric or a rabid communist agitator? It is possible to get some ideas about the former, but the latter, the habits and prejudices and bees-in-bonnet are impossible to divine. A few cautious questions round the profession are called for before the player is contracted.

Turnout is very important too, because it is an indication of the person's general attitude to cleanliness and, in a way, discipline. I remember at one audition when a player arrived late, rubbing his eyes and yawning, and saying that 10.30 was far too early for him to be up and about. He looked as if he had just got out of bed after a night in yesterday's clothes, and he played very badly too. There was simply nothing to recommend in that performance, musically or otherwise.

A clean, alert and smartly-dressed candidate, who looks each of the panel in the eyes, smiles, and quietly goes about his job to the best of his ability, has already earned good marks before a note has been heard. And there is the tuning up. BBC pianos are (purposely it seems) tuned differently in the rehearsal room from the studio where the audition takes place—in every rehearsal room and in every studio. A player who retunes quickly and accurately also gets good marks; one who either does not notice the difference or spends ages getting nowhere, will do himself no good.

At a certain audition some while ago, a man came in before the panel in shirt sleeves and with red braces. He had his sleeves rolled up and spat on his hands before starting his set piece. The panel goggled. What information there was available about the man suggested that he was partly amateur, and had certainly never played in an orchestra. He did not notice that the piano was a good quarter of a tone sharper than the one he had tuned to, and went blithely on to finish his set piece. When he had some sight reading given him, he stared, moved back from the stand, then forward again and said 'What's all this then?' The leader of the orchestra went over to him to discover what was troubling him and found that the man was pointing to a note high up on the leger lines, which he appeared not to recognise at all. The leader explained that it was an E. 'Oh well,' said the man, 'if that's the sort of thing you want, it's not for me. Good morning.' And off he strode. Outside, he declared to those waiting that he had only come up to London at BBC's expense for a night out, and he was going to see all round Soho before he went back on Monday.

And there have been worse cases than that: some of them too pathetic and sad to tell.

Depending upon a player's age, reputation, nature and temperament, he may actually enjoy auditions; or he may hate them so much that he will refuse to do one. If an experienced player had decided to give up the world of sessions, teaching, tours and the odd job here and there in favour of a steady job in an orchestra, or if he is attempting to change orchestras without being in the top flight of players, he will still regard an audition as entirely superfluous. As he is a self-styled 'big-time' player, he merely writes and asks when he can start. His first free date (after a list of supposedly impressive engagements) is so-and-so. The BBC insist on an audition and very often this leads to acrimony, for the player will refuse point blank. Eventually he will realise that unless he appears, he will not get anywhere, so he agrees to go along *last of all* on the day of the audition 'just to meet the panel and chat to them', as it has been put to him. He is also reminded that for his own sake, never mind anybody else's, it is as well that he avoids any possible later criticism that he was not even there. 'No', he is told, he 'cannot actually come on another day because the assessor is not available except then, and the two of them must meet *again*'. They may, or may not know each other. It always works, and the player always brings his instrument along.

He strides into the room brandishing his instrument and declaring that he is short of time, 'Of course I'm not going to play this either,' he emphasises, 'I've just come from . . . and I'm off to . . . by six o'clock, you know the form?' The panel nods enthusiastically, although really they are all bored stiff by this very familiar battle drill.

The man sits down on the edge of his chair which he has pulled away from the music stand towards the panel's table, and glowers at the friendly faces opposite him. They are charming, talk his shop (those who can), and gradually force him to relax. Then somebody asks brightly 'What's your fiddle?' (or whatever instrument it is). No player can resist demonstrating the varnish, the grain, the label inside and the particular merits of his very particular possession, and of course it comes out of its case. After several minutes, if he hasn't already thought of it, the man gets out his bow at another question. And there he is, with his bow in one hand and his fiddle in the other. He looks round and sighs. 'And I suppose you want me to put them together?' he asks, with a faraway look in his eyes. The panel makes disjointed remarks like 'Is it a big sound?' 'How long have you had it?' 'Where did you get it, it's a lovely-looking fiddle.' And 'Let's hear it with the other bow' (a cunning one, this). And so he plays, and the panel have been able to hear him despite his utter refusal to play to them. I'm sure this dodge is as old as the hills, but I've found it to work very well without having had it described by anybody else. Somebody there is sure to be able to play the piano and so (the professional accompanists engaged for the 'normal' candidates not being there) the audition proceeds as normal. The dreadful part comes when this special case is not accepted and it is for the orchestral manager to break the news to him.

It does not follow that because an audition is being held, an appointment will be made. The availability of people to attend varies from day to day, and some excellent person who might be free on a Monday but not on the day of the audition, is not heard, and might be just the right one. So sometimes no recommendation is made. It is the wisest course if the standard of playing is not high enough.

From everybody's point of view it is essential that the panel are visible to each candidate all the time. The BBC used to have a very bad practice of hiding the panel in the studio producer's box, with either the light out or a screen across the glass. The VOICE came through a loud speaker and the whole proceedings were inhuman. In fact several players who experienced this from the wrong end said they did not know whether anybody was there at all, or how frequently they went out for drinks. This does not happen any longer.

ORCHESTRAL ATTENDANTS

Behind the manager, who is himself behind the orchestra, stand the orchestral attendants or 'porters' as they used to be called before they asked to be deprived of their connotation with British Rail. They are a breed all to themselves, a yeoman breed such as was found among the best senior sergeants, chief petty officers

and warrant officers in the wartime services. They are totally
unflappable, can turn their hands to almost anything, are in-
defatigable, have firm loyalties, and possess a strange knowledge of music. Because music is part of their lives, these men
absorb it without understanding it fully, and they also remember
the most extraordinary things, like the number of extra players
which certain works require. Although their lives are only
indirectly related to the music which is played, they are con-
tributing to it, and at the same time are letting music occupy a
little of their own lives. Some of them are able to appreciate good
playing as well as bad, but if questioned about it, they would not
be able to explain how they have got the right answers.

One or two exceptions fall below the extremely high standards
which the majority of these attendants can achieve, and they are
well known. For it is a closed shop in terms of personalities.
They usually meet their opposite numbers from other orchestras
outside concert halls when one orchestra is 'getting-out' as the
other is 'getting-in'. Even if they have not met for six months,
they have heard about each other in between and easily pick up
the threads and exchange news, about their own orchestra (if it
is good) and about the others no matter what they are like.
'Heard about the LPO? No? Bit of trouble in their aeroplane last
week going to China. They were all saying their prayers.' So the
word gets round, often within the week, and news is carried in
the age-old manner from man to man by word of mouth, as the
vans carrying the instruments meet and part and their occupants
act as twentieth-century orchestral messengers.

A good orchestral attendant (and most of the forty or so are
really good) not only knows his own job backwards, but needs to
be something of a psychologist to follow the ever-changing
moods and whims of the players. The present generation of
senior orchestral attendants has learned its first lessons in the
services and consequently is composed of well-disciplined men.
They have little time or sympathy for the namby-pamby creatures
among the musicians, who probably vary little from their fathers
before the wartime NCO's, now attendants, moulded them
(metaphorically speaking) twenty-five years ago. Then the
NCO's knocked them into shape and made men out of jelly, but
of course they cannot do this to their sons now, much as the
temptation is there and the toes of their right feet itch. The

orchestral attendant can go no further than to express an opinion about his musicians, quite often in the most direct and Anglo-Saxon manner possible, and always at a well-chosen moment when the subject is entirely in the wrong and cannot object too forcibly. The attendant will judge an atmosphere and comment on it to the manager, if they are on ideal terms, even to the extent of warning him that it might be a good idea to show himself.

Some attendants are regarded by the players as sources of wisdom, as well as of information, and will be approached at an early stage to hear their reaction to some ploy or personal decision. Because a good attendant is regarded partly as management, and is thought to be on close terms with the manager, his advice can be worth having because of the possibility that he may pass on the information. If this is what the player wants, it is indeed a good idea, but only in the short term, because managers are never that foolish that they cannot see through a simple plan. The attendant can even be primed to drop a hint or to state a preference or an idea as his own in the right quarter, of course. He will do so, if he agrees. If he does not agree, he will make it quite clear that it is not his business to interfere.

The attendants' official duties are not concerned with the players' machinations at all. First and foremost they are charged with packing the instruments into the van, accompanying it to the next hall, and then laying out the platform for the rehearsal. This means putting chairs and music stands in exactly the right position according to the works being played and for exactly the appropriate number and kind of players. They know by instinct the distances required between chairs, and their positioning *vis-à-vis* one another; and they then bring in and lay out the larger instruments which may have travelled in the van that one of them has driven himself. Many musicians tend to carry their own instruments about with them if they are violinists, violists, flautists, oboists or clarinettists. Cellists are variable and in any case most musicians try to get as much extra work as they can. The very busy ones never use the instrument van at all, even though they may play the harp, double bass, or percussion. In the latter case they will have their own van, possibly driven by their own employee (known as their 'roady'). A successful harp player will have a shooting brake more likely than not, so that he can get the instrument in and out, if need be, on his own. The more important or affluent a musician (the two do not necessarily go together at first) the more likelihood there is of his having two instruments or even more. If he has a regular date to play once a week outside his normal orchestral commitments, he may well leave the other instrument there, unless he keeps it at home. At all events this will make it possible for him to be far more flexible in the way he plans his work, and he must keep the orchestral attendant fully in the picture about where 'the other' instrument is. There are times when it may have to be got at short notice for the orchestral concert. And then money has to change hands.

The orchestral attendants have got to be present, or within call, throughout all sessions in case, for example, alterations are required to the seating or there is an accident. The senior attendant quite often acts as the conductor's personal servant, fetches and carries for him, helps him to change, makes him feel supported. He also keeps fans out after the concert, and wives too. But do not imagine that the attendants are sitting close by the platform, on the *qui vive*. They will be in the local, or wherever beer is to be found within the shortest possible distance. In the more modern, and certainly enlightened concert halls like the Royal Festival Hall and the Fairfield Halls at Croydon, and the Royal Albert Hall, too, there is a staff bar, so that the thirsty ones do not have to leave the building. Even so, the nearest local is always well known, and it is probably the librarian who will fetch the attendants if they are needed.

THE LIBRARIAN

The orchestral attendants work, or should work closely with the librarian, a very important member of the supporting team. He is usually a retired orchestral player, even from the orchestra which he now serves in another capacity, and he can read music fluently, understands orchestral routines perfectly and may even still play some delicate instrument like the contra bassoon or basset horn. It is thus likely that his services as a player may still be called on from time to time. He is responsible for hiring all scores and parts for forthcoming rehearsals and concerts, if he is the librarian for one of the independent symphony orchestras; and he is also responsible for seeing that these parts are clean and fit to play from. Sometimes when the only available parts are across the world, or the London or Manchester or Glasgow agent is unable to supply them at the right time, and they eventually arrive by air the day before rehearsals start, the librarian wishes that he was back in the orchestra as a player. He has then very likely to sit up all night, going over the parts, and when in doubt as to the exact note in the middle of a mess of pencil-lead, he has to check it with the score. In this case one of the music publishers may lend a hand, although it is not wise to count on it.

So a good librarian quietly and efficiently brings up score after score, part after part, not bothering to tell anybody of the trouble he has had, the midnight oil he has burnt, or the near misses that would have otherwise resulted in a change of programme.

All this presupposes a knowledge by the music librarian of music publishers, the personalities there, and also of the individual works. Whereas the orchestral attendants' knowledge of them is curious and flimsy, the librarian has a keen and close acquaintanceship with every player's part. If there are orchestral songs in a concert, the librarian has to get not one set of parts, but possibly three, each in a different key, to suit the possible requirements of the singer on a day when he or she may not feel able to tackle that top C. Better make it the set of parts in B. 'No in B♭,' says the conductor, 'she won't know as she's singing without a score.' The librarian has a better idea. 'Give her the album with the song in B,' he says. 'She hasn't got perfect pitch, so she will think she's a semi-tone higher than she really is.' And so it is agreed, and the concert is a huge success.

Recently a rare and unpublished work, Delius's opera *The Magic Fountain*, which was composed some eighty years ago, came to light and was considered for performance. Because the manuscript score seemed to be in rather a mess, a musician, acting as music librarian, took a look at it and began to get it into shape. He discovered, to his great surprise, that the composer had written the clarinet line above the oboes throughout. Furthermore he had added several pages at a later date on which, meantime, and differently from the bulk of the score, he had decided to write the trumpet part in C and not in F, as he had done before. To make matters worse, he had only indicated the instrumentation on the left-hand page, and the right-hand one carried across—most of the time. When a score is photostatted, the two pages which make an opening are done together, after which the page of photostat is folded down the middle. Now what was the right-hand page becomes a left-hand page, and all these right-hand pages lacked the instrumentation. There was a great deal to be done before this score was ready for copying. Had it been left as it was, it is doubtful whether any copyist would have taken it on; and this may explain why little interest had been shown in the score for all those years.

The librarian's job is not entirely finished, however, even when he has all the parts in his hand. He then places them on the correct stands throughout the orchestra and passes the full score to the conductor. At rehearsals, the players will frequently be marking the parts with detailed notes, and after the performance they all go back to the librarian. Ideally he should rub out all the pencil-marks, but in practice there is no time for this. So parts arrive with another orchestra's markings, and go away again with different ones, often contradicting what was there before. There will come a time when, with much use, a set of parts is found to be illegible, and then there is a scene.

Before the last war, Serge Koussevitsky, ex-double bass virtuoso and later resident conductor of the Boston Symphony Orchestra, came over to London to conduct another orchestra here. He always conducted from memory, not because he had to, but because Toscanini did, and anything which was good enough for Toscanini was good for Koussevitsky. Unfortunately his memory was not nearly as accurate as the Italian's. Koussevitsky brought all the parts with him from Boston for his London concert, every one marked exactly according to his wishes. This was a very good idea because it saved a lot of rehearsal time, and smacked of good organisation. However the viola players in the London orchestra discovered at a certain place in an exceedingly often-played symphony that their parts had the wrong clef indicated, and it had never been noticed. They said nothing to Koussevitsky, but after the performance when they handed back their parts, wrote on every one:

'Get in the right clef, Boston!'

8

BBC ORCHESTRAS

THE BBC ORCHESTRAS ARE THE ONLY MUSICAL BANDS IN the United Kingdom to be paid like civil servants, whether they are working or not; to be given four weeks' paid holiday a year; and to be obliged to join a pension scheme. Such an enviable situation might be expected to attract the finest orchestral players in the British Isles—and in Europe since 1 January 1973 —but this is far from being the case. Many of the principal players are of good, solid quality, but they vary considerably within the twelve orchestras of the BBC.

The reasons for continued upsets in the BBC orchestras can probably be laid at three doors: the very frailty of human nature, so apparent in musicians, which makes them listen to and absorb rumours about Utopian conditions in the big wide world outside the BBC; the trouble makers and militants (present everywhere in this imperfect world); and the Musicians' Union. Let us examine these three areas separately.

Players who entered a BBC orchestra in their young days have been glad of the security while they bought a car, got married, started a mortgage, raised a family, and even acquired a better instrument. Then, while all this was going on, they received an offer from one of the big orchestras. At this juncture the player might well have been counselled by his wife not to risk their future by stepping into the unknown from reasonable security. So possibly after some considerable wrangling and heartsearching, after arguments at home and everywhere else, he stayed put. Of course he told the BBC about the offer, and used it as a lever to get a higher salary if he stayed; and depending on the financial situation of the BBC at the time (and that is never very good) he either got a small rise, or his bluff was called by the management. But no such offer came again: 'Old So-and-So doesn't want to leave the BBC, you know,' the word got round. 'He's not really the right sort to be anywhere else but under

128

Auntie's skirts . . .' The musical world came to the wrong conclusion that he was not interested. Of course he was, and he hung on and hung on, dropping hints when he realised that there was no point in applying any more for other jobs inside the BBC. So he stayed put, year after weary year, watching the standard of living going up and his own going down, putting up with the same battered old car, and becoming more and more embittered as he ploughed himself deeper into his own rut. Opting for security which his wife found so attractive years ago, was the end of our unfortunate player's potential distinguished career. Restriction is the most dangerous opponent to an ambitious musician, for unless he knocks about a bit and finds out exactly what suits his own particular talents, and where they in turn are best suited, he can never be a rounded and complete person, let alone a finished musician. So this man never ceases to bore other people by the story of his past: how he turned down the LSO or the LPO because of course they didn't appreciate how he . . . and on and on he goes. Self-defence and disappointment are always evident in stories like these because they are thrown at one, uninvited. Such an experience can make the player divert his energies and frustrations into other likely channels such as becoming the chairman of his orchestral committee, and lording it over his colleagues in matters of intelligence and learning. In other words he finishes up by becoming a great nuisance to everybody, his colleagues no less, because of his warped outlook. What he never considers is the possibility that he might have made a hash of the other job and been without any income at all. The BBC may often seem very boring and very tame, but it is also very cosy, and it is almost impossible to get the sack.

Another kind of trouble-maker, while we are on the subject, is the practical joker, who can very often cause more distress than he either intends or wishes, by spreading rumours that are known to be false, just to watch other people's faces, and see how far it gets before it is discredited. These awkward people enjoy ribbing conductors and causing pinpricks of annoyance for the sake of a temporary laugh or for a personal gain.

Militants have all got the same characteristics under most conditions of work, in that they place themselves before their colleagues and their craft, and the Union Rules before all else.

They are something like religious maniacs in the way they take every word in the book of rules as gospel; or like a conductor who erroneously believes that the full score is a blueprint for the composition, not a map to be interpreted according to his own experience and wisdom. But because a high proportion of musicians are quiet, pleasant and good-natured people who don't like making a fuss, they are forced along by the militants, like sheep. An iron fist goes a long way in dealing with docile people, whoever they may be, and don't the wielders know it! A few years ago the Musicians' Union called a full scale meeting in London about awarding *ad hoc* players an increase, so that as extras or deputies employed by the BBC they would get nearly 50 per cent more than their salaried colleagues, per session. This meeting was so poorly and apathetically attended by BBC musicians that their counter-vote was swept away by the overwhelming majority who, of course, would profit from carrying it. Of course this caused a great deal of bitterness, especially when the freelance players boasted about the enhanced value of each session, quoting pounds sterling. The BBC musicians became more childish than usual and, forgetting their contracts duly signed (but one doubts whether fully read and understood) began to blame everybody in sight: the BBC management, their union, their freelance colleagues. It goes back to the old concept: if you have agreed to do something and have set your name to it, and then you find you don't like it, you can't blame others.

Many people consider that the Musicians' Union and particularly its London Branch has a lot to answer for over this agreement for different rates of pay for the same job. So there is equal pay for men and women musicians, that's a start; and BBC orchestral players consider that although the freelance player lives far more on his nerves, he doesn't really deserve a bit extra to protect himself and his family against the fact that he may not be working at all next week. Primarily the freelance player wants to have a freelance life. Providing he has acquired and maintains his contacts, continues to play well, is punctual, friendly and has a wife or an Ansafone to take messages at any hour of the day or night, he will not want for work. And once he gets into the gramophone record and film sessions, he can turn over £7,000 or £8,000 a year without going in for heart attacks. But if he becomes greedy, he will work for longer hours and at places too far removed from each other than will be good for him. While the Musicians' Union prevents BBC musicians from playing three sessions in one day as a matter of routine (although it can be arranged specially for two or three occasions in one year), the freelance player does not regard the day as well spent if he has not got three sessions in. Of course a BBC player may well do a concert or a session for some other orchestra after two sessions in the studio. Does he mind? Not at all? Does the union mind? Oh no, good luck to him. Does the BBC mind? They turn a blind eye. But let the BBC try to work him for nine hours a day, and that instantly becomes sweated labour. So it's all rather a case of what's yours is mine, and what's mine's my own, so far as the union is concerned.

Then, there is the positively iniquitous situation, started by the BBC Symphony Orchestra, of co-principals. This was the appointment of two different players of high calibre to share the leading and principal posts. So in effect all these appointments were made at the full rate, yet their holders needed to work for only half the time. When they were not working for the BBC they were working for somebody else, and thus collected BBC money and outside money for all their outside sessions. The idea behind this was to attract better players to the BBC Symphony Orchestra, but of course the other orchestras in London were forced to adopt a similar practice and a huge spiral started in principals' salaries throughout the profession. Naturally this pleased the union, because as the principal rates increased dramatically, so the rank and file—not to mention the sub-principals—demanded more money to even things up a bit.

Because the BBC is by far the largest employer of musicians in Britain, with a statutory 600 plus the Academy in Bristol, their needs must be the main target for the Musicians' Union. While the top management of the BBC dropped a colossal brick in 1970 with their *Broadcasting in the Seventies*, a disastrous document, musically speaking, if ever there was one, the MU do not always have such ready ammunition as this for an assault. This document suggested, among other things, the dissolution of some of the BBC orchestras, thus contravening an agreement with the union whereby the BBC should always employ not less than 600 musicians. Conversely, though, the union has broken its side of some agreements. It is invariably the same piece of battle drill on their part. We want more money, much more money for *our* players and shorter hours. And by and large, a little bit at a time, wearing away the patience and charm and undoubted commonsense and goodwill of the BBC's management, they are moving towards a situation when a symphony by Beethoven—let alone one by Mahler or Bruckner—will be too long to record at a single session in the studio and therefore too expensive to broadcast. At this rate all the players will be collecting princely salaries for the privilege of working once a week—at the most, and that will be straining it. A *reductio ad absurdum*, you will say, and let us, at any rate, hope that it is. For musicians are in the main excellent people whose whole life is bound up with their instrument, themselves and music. It would be unthinkable, taken to a logical conclusion, for a musician of today to be prevented from playing. But then we do not know for how long this noble breed is born to continue.

The Musicians' Union has a governing body of brothers who have given up, or been given up by, their trade to go into the office and run the union and the affairs of 9,000 British musicians. A committe man may be a good, well-meaning and conscientious person; he may on the other hand be a senior member of the Communist party with axes to grind at every blink; or else he may be hopeless as an administrator and manage to gum up the works in a shocking manner. I have heard a union representative of an orchestra announce to his colleagues that something like five telephone calls and three letters have gone unanswered when he has tried to communicate with his local branch over a matter which the orchestra considered to be of great importance. In his capacity of go-between on behalf of the orchestra, one was not surprised that he spoke from the heart when he said 'I'm fed up with the union. They're hopeless to get anything definite out of.'

This conflicts strangely with the union's holier than thou attitude towards the BBC management. To the union, the scandalous underpayment to their—the union's—musicians, the long hours, the poor allowances and squalid conditions in which their—the union's players have to work for their pittance, should all be remedied here and now. It is significant that the union claims ownership of the musicians although in the past the labourer was worthy only of his hire and so responsible to the person or organisation who paid him.

Musicians in the BBC are cosseted and pampered like nowhere else. Because the management dislikes having to go through the appeasing motions whenever the union raises a point of order with them, they tend to bend over backwards to avoid any sort of confrontation. They scarcely ever need a union at all, so fair are the methods of treatment, so scrupulously are complaints looked into and dealt with. It is in the outside orchestras where instant dismissal for very little reason may occasionally require a mediator, yet there the directors of the orchestra are all members of the same union, and the situation is completely different.

Nowadays each BBC musician bears a prime loyalty to his art, and then afterwards, and a long way behind, a grudging admission to the employer for payment, bound up with grouses and complaints. 'I don't belong to the BBC!' more than one musician on the staff of the BBC has said with shocked voice and expression, 'I only play for them because I've got to.' You notice the 'them'. Back to that proverbial red rag, the contract, which BBC musicians positively loathe to hear mentioned, worst of all brought up as a reason for having something done. This is a 'first-call' contract, meaning that the BBC has first call on each player's time. Only by asking for permission to be away and getting it can he officially avoid playing at an advertised session. And the word 'officially' is important because there are those players who go sick for no reason at all and either have the day off with the family, or, more likely, do a date in a reasonably secluded place where there is very little likelihood of their being noticed. A little of this behaviour can lead to bravado, carelessness and then exposure. For not only has a BBC musician three days' grace of illness before he need provide a doctor's certificate, he will be unable to prevent himself from boasting to one or two friends about how well he did the BBC for a couple of days. The few drinks that he buys his friends while they joke about it will minimise the security aspect of his ill-found behaviour, and he will be marked.

It needs an immense amount of proof on the part of management before they stir their stumps and come out with an accusation. The union is always invoked by the player, and the union will ask for the evidence, will go through it minutely, and will try—as any good defending counsel will try—to find a loophole in the evidence. If the dice fall against the player, he will hope to be summarily dismissed (if it is beyond the stage of a bad report and ticking-off). There is no other form of punishment. If he resigns, and honour tends to be something of an old-fashioned commodity in this respect, he goes almost at once and receives no lump-sum from the BBC by way of redundancy payment. If he is pushed out he gets paid this sum as well as getting back all that he has put into the fund for his pension. Even if the copy-book is seriously blotted, the punishment is not severe, and at the same time the culprit may stir up a lot of sympathy and support from other members of his orchestra if he plays his cards properly.

Musicians who have been in a military band (but not the wartime kind) or have been to university, or have come into orchestral life in mature middle age, are most valuable in an orchestra. In the case of a man this latter incidence is very rare, though most refreshing when it happens. Such stabilising influ-ence is of immense value to the other members of the orchestra, who have perhaps relied for years upon the mangled judgements of such a man whose unfortunate career you will have read about on page 129.

Those musicians who found themselves at a critical point in their careers at the outbreak of war were, like any other artists, faced with the alternative of taking it soft, or of putting the maximum of effort into their wartime service. Indeed this also applied in some cases to peacetime soldiers who suddenly found themselves faced with the unpleasant possibility of actually having to fight and to get dirty. I well remember a Grenadier Guards captain who positively blanched on the morning of 3 September 1939 and made absolutely certain that he got posted to a string of non-combatant units. But that did not prevent him from being promoted to a high rank. Yet while it was not quite so common to find pacifists in the Army, there were many to be found in the artistic professions. As it was said at the time: 'Many budding recruits for a National Socialist England are waiting among the country's artists.' Perhaps it is a short step from loyalty to employer and loyalty to King and Country: as short a step as disloyalty to both. Suffice it to say, however, that sitting on the fence in a military band until the Battle of Britain was won was the lot of some of our finest orchestral players, soloists and others, to whom military discipline was anathema and everybody else's main objective of winning the war a dreadful bore because of the restrictions which they had to suffer.

For the usual run of musician, the normal player, is fond of his creature comforts. Although the brass players really do need several pints after a long blow, this does not prevent the string and woodwind players from drinking as much, even in hard liquor. And there is always the local for BBC musicians. In central London it is easy: Aeolian Hall, the Paris Cinema, the Playhouse and Broadcasting House offer no problems; neither do the studios of the regional BBC orchestras. Maida Vale is tiresome, though. This is the home of the BBC Symphony Orchestra and the nearest 'boozer' is a fair step away. Nor is the canteen within the building licensed. This building, by the way, has at different times been a laundry and a skating-rink. 'Not so different now', it has been observed. If you walk (or run) from the Maida Vale Studios to the Shirland Arms (tatty and uninviting and with an excruciating juke-box always on the go) that is the nearest; but the George is much better though half as far away again. Some of the musicians drive there.

Another George is the most celebrated BBC pub of all. When the Queen's Hall (accent on *Queen's*, by the way) was intact, the George in Mortimer Street was the nearest. And because it used to take so long to prise the solid drinkers out of it in Sir Henry Wood's time, it became known as 'The Glue-Pot', and still is today, though only out of tradition. One of the older string-players remarked the other day: 'Been to the Glue-Pot lately? How it's changed. Girls are all the rage there now, even invading the quiet haunts of musicians!' Nobody could ever describe the Glue-Pot as 'quiet', but it is the complete re-orientation which, despite its imposing new direction, gave this cellist reason to mourn the passing of the old days with all the nostalgia they still conjure up for him.

In 1930 the BBC Symphony Orchestra was formed and founded by Adrian (seven years later Sir Adrian) Boult, who was then the Head of Music at the BBC as well as this orchestra's conductor. In 1950, Boult was declared too old to

remain with the Corporation, having reached the statutory re-
tiring age of 60, though retirement can be extended 'at the
discretion of the BBC, year by year to maximum age 65'. He
was incensed and knew quite well that he had many more active
years of music-making in him. So in great disgust he left to
spend another quarter of a century conducting elsewhere. He has
never forgotten nor forgiven the Corporation for this, as the
following story will show.

Many years later, Sir Adrian agreed to conduct a concert with
his old orchestra and to rehearse at the main Maida Vale Studio,
No. 1 as it is called. The electric clock directly in front of the
conductor's rostrum (at the back of and above the players) had
stopped, and nobody could be found to adjust it. It had to be an
electrician. Boult said that unless the clock was made to go
again, he would respond to the time on the dial, in which case
the rehearsal would be over in ten minutes. After the orchestral
management had wasted a good deal more time in wondering
how to deal with this unexpected situation, they cut the Gordian
knot by having the hands of the clock removed. Sir Adrian
was now satisfied and the rehearsal proceeded. The hands remained off that clock for very nearly a year.

Sir Adrian's original BBC Symphony Orchestra was probably
the best symphony orchestra in London in 1938, when Toscanini
conducted it during the London Music Festival. During the
war it lost some of them to National Service, was evacuated to
Bedford and then to the West Country, where it played many
concerts that were broadcast to music-starved servicemen in all
theatres of operations.

After Sir Adrian's departure, Malcolm Sargent became the
orchestra's principal conductor and established himself and his
orchestra at the Promenade Concerts like nobody has done
since. After Queen's Hall was destroyed by bombs in 1940, the
Promenade Concerts have been held in the Albert Hall each
summer, and in 1950 William Glock arrived as Controller of
Music. He had been a piano pupil of Schnabel, and had then
played a great part in running Dartington Hall's activities in
Devon. He made enormous changes to the whole pattern of the
BBC's music, emphasising the *avant-garde* and describing the
solid fare of the Three B's as 'Museum Concerts'. While
Sargent was not entirely at home in this kind of new music, there

was no objection to guest conductors coming in and 'doing their thing'. The conductor in this instance was Pierre Boulez, and the thing was still called music.

Many of the orchestral players found the new music hard going, quite contrary to their experience and puzzling in the extreme, because it scarcely ever satisfied them musically. A flute player said that throughout this training and many long years in the profession he had learned how to avoid splitting notes. And now Mr Boulez was asking him to split them. How welcome were Sargent's sessions after a dose of Boulez (or 'Mr Bootlace' as he is nicknamed). Then when Sargent so regrettably and suddenly died, Colin Davis, a young hopeful, was appointed to succeed him.

Davis had started his career as an unexceptional clarinettist, had learned to conduct with small orchestras by giving good and progressive concerts in Chelsea soon after the war. He had suddenly leapt to fame by deputising at very short notice for Klemperer in a performance of *Don Giovanni*. He had been conducting it in his capacity of chief conductor of Sadler's Wells Opera. From then on Colin Davis's career was assured and he got plenty of engagements at home and abroad. The BBC Symphony Orchestra came to him as a stepping-stone, so far as he was concerned, for he never seems to stay long in any one job. He sprang off to be Musical Director at Covent Garden in succession to Sir George Solti, though without the important prop of Peter Hall, who was to have accompanied him to look after the production of opera. Where will he go next? The Metropolitan, New York? There are few places left. Unfortunately, and partly because he is so young, he has not yet acquired the necessary tact and ability to charm musicians. One recalls an occasion when, in front of the whole BBC Symphony Orchestra, he attempted to teach Jack Brymer how to play a certain clarinet phrase in Beethoven's 'Pastoral' Symphony . . . But Colin Davis was a very good conductor of the Last Night of the Proms, a particular role that suits, or can be suited, to only a very few men. Yet he has given this up too. His eccentricities were extended, in his BBC time, to allowing the musicians to wear any old clothes at public concerts on the grounds that this is how they rehearse, and evening dress makes it awkward for them. How strange that this generation of players finds the only identical dress of fifty years ago now in current use to be suddenly 'awkward'! In addition, many people feel that it adds a touch of occasion to a concert when the orchestra are, what we generally accept as properly dressed, as well as it being implied as a compliment to the audience.

In 1966 and 1967, Pierre Boulez was conducting concerts for both the BBC Symphony Orchestra and the LSO, quite clearly canvassing for the conductorship of a London orchestra. The LSO were profoundly put out by his kind of music, which they roundly condemned and detested, and this left the field open to William Glock and the BBC, much to his delight. On 1 Jan 1968 Boulez was appointed Principal Conductor of the BBC Symphony Orchestra and at once began to reconstitute it according to his own requirements. He held auditions for all the players and got rid of those who either did not respond to him, or whom he did not want There is a very strict procedure for auditioning orchestral players at the BBC, when the conductor, leader, section principal, orchestral manager, and possibly other members of management are joined by an independent 'outside' assessor who is a distinguished player of the instrument in question. But in the Boulez régime it is Boulez who says whom he will have and whom he will not have. The remainder of the panel acquiesce.

This leads one to note that the BBC Symphony Orchestra was, is, and probably always will be the Corporation's most privileged orchestra. It is their only symphony orchestra in London, and apart from its players qualifying for the meagre London weighting, they are on the spot to compete in the market-square bartering for top players, which goes on from time to time between all the five symphony orchestras in the metropolis.

When Alan Civil, first horn, announced that he did not wish to stay any longer in the BBC Symphony Orchestra under Boulez, a grand auction took place between this band and the LSO. Civil's going rate was mightily increased, the arguments about who was going to have him went on and on, until he turned his back on them both and became principal horn of the New Philharmonia! Certain players of more than average ability can ask more or less what they want and get it outside. In the BBC it is not so easy because rates are pegged, yet with a little tolerance for 'travelling', this can often swing the scale. But this exacerbates the feelings of the rank and file, even the sub-principals too, who all think they know what their distinguished colleague is taking home even before he gets paid for his many useful 'gigs', done, of course, in his spare time. And these can never be confidential because concerts are advertised and other players will see him there.

It is when one of these exceptional players turns his mind to orchestral politics that things can become dangerous. After the war there were four players in the Royal Philharmonic Orchestra who were known as the 'Royal Family'. When Beecham was not there they completely ruled the orchestra, its soloists and conductors, and managed to do great personal harm to one of them. This was the veteran, Basil Cameron, who was one day rehearsing them for a promenade concert. He said he wanted a certain passage played in a certain way. One of the Royal Family rudely asked 'Why?' Cameron was a little nonplussed, and replied that this was the way in which he wanted it done. The response was that the musicians would play it in their own way. Instead of leaving the rostrum and reporting the incident as he should have done, Cameron got himself bogged down in argument and increasing rudeness, as a result of which he later suffered a nervous breakdown. That 'Royal Family' have long since been dispersed, but every orchestra tends to have its self-styled 'King', sometimes several of them, all working in different directions. The best thing that can be said of this state of affairs is that they quite often cancel out each other's activities, while expending an enormous amount of energy in the process.

The BBC Symphony Orchestra has a hard and fast arrangement with the Royal Festival Hall to give live concerts from there on Wednesdays—not every Wednesday, but probably once a month. This day is theirs by tradition, whereas the four 'outside' orchestras have to haggle and barter for Tuesdays, Thursdays and Sundays throughout the season. You will notice that there is one day of the week less than the number of orchestras wishing to play. Moreover, the BBC Symphony Orchestra always broadcasts its own concerts live, whereas the other orchestras' live broadcasts are few and far between. For many peoples' licence money, music by the LSO, the LPO, the NPO or the RPO would make infinitely preferable listening.

A few years ago the managers of the 'outside' orchestras went to the BBC to make representation about more broadcasts of their concerts. They did not understand the system within the BBC of controllers, heads of departments, chief assistants, planners and producers and all the other titles which are so meaningful inside the BBC, yet so puzzling to everybody outside it. Consequently each member of the BBC team, well and strongly chosen, was able to play a fine game of eluding every question put to them by claiming that this point was not what he was responsible for. It all ended with the declaration that many foreign tapes, 'forced on the BBC by the European Broadcasting Union' must take precedence over London orchestras' concert broadcasts. In fact many of these foreign tapes are of sub-standard material which, although each goes through a system of listening and reporting, are not familiar in atmosphere or as regards the orchestras, soloists and conductors, and merely act as cheap fill-ins.

So all round, the BBC Symphony Orchestra, with its large number of supporting troops in Broadcasting House, has the upper hand, not only over all other orchestras in the Corporation, but to a great extent over its direct competitors in London, and that means in the UK. For let us face it: there is no symphony orchestra outside London which is comparable to the top three within it. One has only to go into the provinces and listen. There are good orchestras there, but not up to the world-class standards that we expect to hear at Festival Hall. This is demonstrably true over matters of string playing, in particular, with its attendant problems of ensemble, intonation and incisiveness. We are shorter of good string players in the whole country than any other department of the orchestra. It is a fact, and you may think it a sad one, that London has undeniably got the cream of the players. Were they to be scattered round Britain more evenly, it would give the varying strata of players below the superlative ones, a better chance of better jobs.

The BBC Northern Orchestra follows the BBC Symphony Orchestra in prestige, although it is rather a long way behind. They are situated in Manchester, where they seem to have been put to diminish the glory and spite the home ground of the Hallé. Or this is what many of the old die-hard supporters of the Hallé say. Yet at the time when the BBC Northern Orchestra was raised, Manchester seemed the best spot, geographically speaking, for a large BBC encampment, whose orchestra would be able 'to serve the North of England'. Needless to say, York-shiremen have never agreed. This orchestra generally plays 'middle of the road Radio 3 symphonic music' to quote the jargon, which William Glock used to describe as fodder for 'museum concerts'. By this he meant Beethoven, Brahms, Haydn, Mozart, Strauss, and Elgar, but not so much Elgar when Barbirolli was with the Hallé. In anybody's terms, this is real, solid, sensible and understandable symphonic fare. Yet *understandable* is not a fashionable tenet at the BBC nowadays among many of its 'serious music' people. However, the Northern Orchestra, the Welsh Orchestra and the Scottish Orchestra, all regional symphony orchestras, are not regarded with anything like the esteem of The Symphony Orchestra, as it is called, the Corporation's showpiece. Whether the new Controller of Music, Robert Ponsonby, who succeeded Sir William Glock in 1973, will think differently, remains to be seen. At all events, Boulez leaves in 1975.

Ernest Roth, that wisest of musical businessmen once said: 'Boulez you may not like, as composer or conductor. But as composer, well he is the best we have got today.' Perhaps in the same way as a nation is said to get its deserts in its parliament, so a broadcasting corporation's orchestra also gets the conductor it deserves.

9

MAIN BRITISH ORCHESTRAS

ROYAL PHILHARMONIC SOCIETY

THE OLDEST ORCHESTRA STILL SURVIVING IN LONDON, the London Symphony Orchestra, is not the oldest concert-giving organisation. This is the Royal Philharmonic Society, which is the second oldest of its kind in the world, junior to the Leipzig Gewandhaus Orchestra (see page 152) by seventy years, but thereafter senior to every other, in Europe and America.

Three musicians called J. B. Cramer, P. A. Corri and William Dance held a meeting at Dance's house, 17 Manchester Square, London, on 24 January 1813, at a time when there was no permanent orchestra in London able to give symphony concerts. Two weeks later, their chairman, Mr Dance, and his colleagues, drew up a constitution which thirty professional London musicians signed, under the title of The Philharmonic Society of London. They gave their first concert on 8 March 1813 at the Argyll Rooms. This hall was burned down in 1830 and stood at the corner of Oxford Street and Argyll Street, where one of the entrances to Oxford Circus underground station is now. It was the Philharmonic Society who commissioned the 'Choral' Symphony from Beethoven for £50 in 1825 and who advanced him £100 two years later to help ease him in his illness. The Society received permission to add 'Royal' to its title in November 1912.

In its early days the orchestra of the Philharmonic Society (not the Philharmonic Orchestra) had no proper conductor as we now know him. The responsibility for direction was split between the leader and the musician who sat at the piano with the full score. This maintained for the seasons 1813–1820 and 1821–1843. After this, conductors have been established as follows:

Mendelssohn (5		Frederic Cowen	1912–1913
concerts out of 8)	1844	Willem Mengelberg	1913–1914
Henry Bishop	1845	Balfour Gardiner	,,
Ignaz Moscheles	,,	V. I. Safonov	,,
Michael Costa	1846–1854	Sir Thomas Beecham	1914–1915
Richard Wagner	1855	V. I. Safonov	,,
W. Sterndale Bennett	1856–1866	Percy Pitt	,,
W. G. Cusins	1867–1883	Sir Thomas Beecham	,,
Four conductors	1884	Sir Thomas Beecham	1916–1917
Arthur Sullivan	1885–1887	Landon Ronald	,,
Frederic Cowen	1888–1892	Sir Thomas Beecham	1917–1918
Alexander Mackenzie	1893–1899	Landon Ronald	,,
Frederic Cowen	1900–1907	Landon Ronald	1918–1919
Henry J. Wood	1908	Adrian Boult	,,
Frederic Cowen	,,	Geoffrey Toye	,,
Landon Ronald	,,	Albert Coates	1919–1920
Artur Nikisch	,,	Geoffrey Toye	,,
Artur Nikisch	1908–1909	Adrian Boult	,,
Henry J. Wood	,,	Charles K. Scott	,,
Landon Ronald	,,	Landon Ronald	,,
Two others	,,	Albert Coates	1920–1921
Landon Ronald	1909–1910	Hamilton Harty	,,
Luigi Mancinelli	,,	Albert Coates	1921–1922
Artur Nikisch	,,	Adrian Boult	,,
Sir Edward Elgar	,,	Frank Bridge	,,
Bruno Walter	,,	Albert Coates	1922–1923
Albert Coates	1910–1911	Landon Ronald	,,
V. I. Safonov	,,	Eugene Goossens Jr.	,,
Artur Nikisch	,,	Albert Coates	1923–1924
Sir Edward Elgar	,,	Ernest Ansermet	,,
Thomas Beecham	,,	Sir Landon Ronald	,,
Two others	,,	Wilhelm Furtwängler	,,
Sir Edward Elgar	1911–1912	Eugene Goossens Jr.	,,
Landon Ronald	,,	Felix Weingartner	,,
Alexander Mackenzie	,,	Wilhelm Furtwängler	1924–1925
Artur Nikisch	,,	Bruno Walter	,,
Percy Pitt	,,	Eugene Goossens Jr.	,,
Willem Mengelberg	,,	Ernest Ansermet	,,
Sir Charles Stanford	,,	Felix Weingartner	,,
V. I. Safonov	,,	Paul Klenau	,,
V. I. Safonov	1912–1913	Malcolm Sargent	,,
Landon Ronald	,,	Albert Coates	1925–1926
Willem Mengelberg	,,	Sir Edward Elgar	,,
Percy Pitt	,,	Malcolm Sargent	,,

M. Rhène-Baton	1925–1926	Fernandez Arbós	1926–1927
Paul Klenau	,,	Pierre Monteux	,,
Sir Landon Ronald	,,	Frank Bridge	,,
Sir Henry Wood	1926–1927	Sir Hugh Allen	,,
Bruno Walter	,,	Sir Thomas Beecham	1928–1930

The future of the Royal Philharmonic was in considerable doubt in 1927, partly due to the collapse of a scheme to buy Queen's Hall on behalf of the Society by public subscription; also on account of cherished plans to form a new orchestra in collaboration with the BBC. These plans came to nothing. And when the BBC formed its own Symphony Orchestra in 1930, the Orchestra of the Royal Philharmonic Society ceased to exist. Then, in 1932 Sir Thomas Beecham founded the London Philharmonic Orchestra (note the middle word of the title) with which he sustained the Society concerts until 1939, when he withdrew from all association with the LPO. In this year it established itself on a self-governing basis (see LPO on page 145). Since the last war the Royal Philharmonic Society has found an orchestra to present its concerts (usually only two or three a year) under its banner, but has not had its own orchestra with which to do so.

Two disconnected though important events of the Society occurred in 1813 and 1934. In 1813, with the Society's formation a standard orchestral pitch was adopted, called New Philharmonic Pitch or Diapason Normal. In this, A = 439 cps; B♭ = 465 cps and C = 522 cps, all at 68°F. The other event was the first round table conference of all London Orchestral Concert Societies in 1934. There had been a control committee between the Royal Philharmonic Society and the embryonic London Philharmonic Orchestra from 1930, but now this all-embracing membership included representatives from the BBC, the LPO, the LSO, the Philharmonic Society and Sir Robert Mayer's Children's Concerts. It was undoubtedly the forerunner of the present London Orchestral Concerts Board (see p. 108).

London Symphony Orchestra (LSO) was formed in 1904 from among members of the Queen's Hall Orchestra. These men believed that they should be allowed to employ deputies, which Henry Wood disallowed. So they seceded and while Wood knew he was right to maintain his decision, he was present at the

LSO's first concert on 9 June 1904, and applauded vigorously. Richter was the first conductor. The orchestra has been run ever since as a 'commonwealth' with the musicians electing their own board of directors from within their numbers (for a year at a time) and employing an outside administrator to organise their affairs for them, although he is not a member of the board, rather a servant of the orchestra.

Conductors have been too numerous to mention; and although Richter was principal conductor between 1904 and 1911, it was the policy to acquire the best talent available, not only in conductors but also among soloists and orchestral musicians. Until 1939, the orchestra fulfilled annual engagements at the Three Choirs Festival and at Leeds, but since then it has been Edinburgh and, for some years, Daytona Beach, Florida. The orchestra frequently tours abroad and has been able to maintain its strong reputation as well as to survive financial and other troubles many times in its long existence.

The LSO was probably at its strongest under Ernest Fleischmann's general managership in the 1960s, for his persuasive abilities put the orchestra into first place without his having the total personality of a Beecham or a Legge.

Of late, the principal conductors have been Josef Krips, Antal Dorati, Pierre Monteux, Istvan Kertesz, and now it is André Previn.

London Philharmonic Orchestra (LPO) was formed by Sir Thomas Beecham in 1932 (see p. 144). Under Beecham they not only gave concerts, visited Nazi Germany, and played in the pit at Covent Garden during the opera season, but steadily built up a reputation before the public and in the making of gramophone records. After Beecham, their most significant conductors have been Sir Adrian Boult, Eduard van Beinum and its present one, Bernard Haitink. The LPO occupy the pit at Glyndebourne during their season in the summer every year. They are the only London orchestra whose chief administrator is also a member of the board of directors.

New Philharmonia Orchestra (NPO) was formed as a self-governing organisation by the members of the Philharmonia Orchestra when Walter Legge decided to relinquish control of them or to support them financially any longer. This was in 1966, when they were the première orchestra in London. With a good deal of public goodwill they have managed to keep in line with the other main London orchestras, although recently they have had conductor difficulties. Walter Legge had introduced such men as Karajan, Cantelli, Giulini and Klemperer to London with the Philharmonia Orchestra, and it was Klemperer who became principal conductor until his retirement in 1972. Giulini did not stay for long, and Lorin Maazel's appointment was not a success.

Royal Philharmonic Orchestra (RPO) was founded by Sir Thomas Beecham in 1946, when the war was over and he had no orchestra of his own, having removed himself from the LPO in 1939. He maintained complete rule over the RPO and gave many concerts tied in with gramophone record recordings. Under Beecham it was a highly successful unit and established itself in the pit at Glyndebourne each season. On Beecham's death in 1961, Kempe became conductor in chief (as one of Beecham's last wishes) but he is unable to spare the time to be in London very much. The orchestra looked as if it might be forced into liquidation, while a scheme to deprive it of its title 'Royal' was defeated partly through an active campaign and public support. In common with the three other London orchestras, the RPO became a self-governing body and pulled itself up by its bootstraps. It often gives concerts of works of a more popular nature than its other colleagues do, even of specially commissioned compositions containing jazz or pop elements. It usually tours the USA once a year, making one-night stands in a great number of cities all over the country.

BBC Symphony Orchestra: see pp. 136–141.

The English Chamber Orchestra, the *London Sinfonietta* the *English Sinfonia* and the *London Mozart Players* are, by definition of their titles, not full-scale symphony orchestras, and while I do not intend in any way to denigrate them, I feel that this is not the place to describe them.

New Queen's Hall Orchestra. There are two other orchestras which have figured largely in London's orchestral annals, and while they no longer exist, some mention of them is necessary to fill in the gaps. *The (New) Queen's Hall Orchestra* was formed in 1895 as the Queen's Hall Orchestra in order to give promenade concerts. Robert Newman was its energetic manager, and Henry J. Wood its conductor. As a result of the policy and the popularity of Wood, the Orchestra then gave other concerts from 1897, and from 1902 they were managed by a syndicate, and from 1915 Messrs Chappell's took them over. The formation of the London Philharmonic Orchestra and especially the BBC Symphony Orchestra two years earlier in 1930, squeezed the New Queen's Hall Orchestra out of existence. In 1927 the BBC had taken over Queen's Hall from Chappell's, when they decided to relinquish it, and continued to be responsible for the Proms there until the Hall was destroyed by enemy action in May 1941. The 'New' in the Orchestra's title came about in 1904, when Wood was obliged to recruit a large number of new members. (See under LSO above.) Henry Wood was its conductor throughout its life.

The New Symphony Orchestra (The Royal Albert Hall Orchestra) must have been the only orchestra in the world to possess two names. Originally formed as the New Symphony Orchestra in 1905, it gave its first concerts at the Coronet Theatre, Notting Hill Gate under Evlyn Howard Jones. Beecham then became the conductor and toured with the orchestra in 1906, but in order to avoid his normal procedure of monopolising the orchestra and controlling it autocratically, it became a limited company in 1907. A long provincial tour was then undertaken starring the violinist Jan Kubelik and with Landon Ronald conducting. From 1909, Ronald was the permanent conductor, and remained so until 1919. After the New Symphony Orchestra's London occupation of Queen's Hall between 1909–1914, they continued their series of Sunday afternoon concerts at the Royal Albert Hall that had begun and been continued since 1909 and until the season of 1918–1919. In 1920 they gave four more series of Sunday concerts under the title of Royal Albert Hall Orchestra, and made a number of important recordings under Landon Ronald with this name. The orchestra went under in the late 1920s due to the general upheavals of the time. (See under *New Queen's Hall Orchestra* above).

MAIN ORCHESTRAS OUTSIDE LONDON

Bournemouth Symphony Orchestra. Of our municipal orchestras, the senior is the *Bournemouth Symphony.* With the help of the Corporation of Bournemouth, it was raised and trained by Dan Godfrey in 1893. Today they are the only active orchestra to serve the West of England (save for the Academy of the BBC, formerly the BBC Training Orchestra) and they also provide a smaller orchestra called the Bournemouth Sinfonietta. Their conductors have been:

(Sir) Dan Godfrey	1893–1934
Richard Austin	1934–1939
No orchestra during the war	
Rudolf Schwarz	1949–1951
Charles Groves	
as Musical Director	1951–1954
as Principal Conductor	1954–1961
Constantin Silvestri	1961–1969
Paavo Berglund	1972 to date

The Hallé Orchestra. On New Year's Day 1858, a concert was held in Manchester by the Gentlemen's Concert Orchestra in the Free Trade Hall. This proved to be the beginning of the Hallé Orchestra, since the body of amateurs had been trained by Charles Hallé. Hallé had a precocious talent as a child pianist and, having taken lessons in conducting in Germany and Paris, he came to England in 1843, finally settling in Manchester in 1848. His Gentlemen's Orchestra was formed in connection with the Manchester Exhibition of 1857. He was knighted in 1888 and died in 1895, remaining conductor of his orchestra until the end. The list of conductors of the Hallé Orchestra is:

(Sir) Charles Hallé	1858–1895
different conductors	1895–1898
Hans Richter	1898–1911
Michael Balling	1911–1914
Sir Thomas Beecham	1914–1919
(Sir) Hamilton Harty	1920–1933
Sir Thomas Beecham	
and guest conductors,	
mainly Malcolm Sargent	1933–1943

John Barbirolli 1943–1970
Maurice Handford (as associate) 1966–1971
James Loughran 1971 to date

Royal Liverpool Philharmonic Orchestra as it is now called, has always been part of the (Royal) Philharmonic Society of Liverpool. Although the Society was formed as long ago as 1840 and organised a preponderance of choral concerts, there was enough talent and support to enable the Society to form an orchestra and to build its own hall, the Philharmonic Hall in 1849. This was destroyed by fire in 1933, and rebuilt six years later. The new hall survived the blitz of Liverpool, and is still used today, although it does not look new, nor are its amenities as 'new and modern' as when it was built. The orchestra was not on a full-time basis until 1943, and it is interesting to note that while other orchestras shut up shop during the war, Liverpool's went from strength to strength. The Society and the orchestra were honoured by being able to call themselves 'Royal' during John Pritchard's tenure; and the present conductor, Charles Groves, was knighted in the Queen's New Year's Honours of 1973. Although there was no permanent conductor of the orchestra until 1940, and guest conductors had been the order of the day until then, the list of them since 1940 is as follows:

Malcolm Sargent 1940–1949
Hugo Rignold 1948–1954
Efrem Kurz and John Pritchard 1955–1957
John Pritchard 1957–1963
(Sir) Charles Groves 1963 to date

City of Birmingham Symphony Orchestra. In 1918 a local pianist and choral conductor called Appleby Matthews launched a series of Sunday concerts of orchestral works, entirely at his own expense and risk. They proved so successful that a grant from the city rates was approved, due in some measure to the campaigning of Neville Chamberlain, and many private donations also swelled the funds. The orchestra was formed in 1920 and its inaugural concert was conducted by the then Master of the King's Musick, Sir Edward Elgar, who lived near by. The orchestra has always run at a loss, although the BBC came to the rescue in 1935 by subsidising a contingent from it to be part of the Midland Region station's music department, from which it made regular broadcasts. This and the opportunities for the players to work together more frequently, helped the orchestra to survive the somewhat sporadic pattern of concert-giving up to that time. The orchestra is now completely divorced from the BBC and gives concerts throughout the Midlands as well as in Birmingham. The principal conductors have been:

Appleby Matthews	1920–1924
(Sir) Adrian Boult	1924–1930
Leslie Heward	1930–1943
George Weldon	1943–1951
Rudolf Schwarz	1951–1957
André Panufnik	1957–1959
Sir Adrian Boult	1959–1960
Hugo Rignold	1960–1968
Louis Frémaux	1969 to date

Scottish National Orchestra was formed in Glasgow in 1874 as the Choral Union Orchestra. A rival concern, calling itself the Scottish Orchestra Co. Ltd., was brought into full partnership in 1894 and their united forces were called the Glasgow Choral and Orchestral Union. One of the earliest of many reputable conductors was Willem Kes who, in 1895, when he joined them, had just completed seven seasons as the founder conductor of the Amsterdam Concertgebouw Orchestra (q.v.) As the Scottish Orchestra it survived the 1914–18 war with difficulty, and remained in the 1930s only through the efforts of such great musical personalities as John Barbirolli, George Szell and others who gave guest performances. In 1945 the orchestra was wound up, but reformed in July 1950 as the Scottish National Orchestra, and with Scottish Arts Council support. It has not ceased to give concerts in the meanwhile, when it was supported first by the Glasgow Choral Union and then by the Arts Council. Its conductors have been:

George Henschel	1893–1895
Willem Kes	1895–1898
Wilhelm Bruch	1898–1900
Frederic Cowen	1900–1910
Emil Mlynarski	1910–1916
Concerts abandoned	1916–1919

Landon Ronald	1919–1923
Guest Conductors	1923–1925
Vaclav Talich	1926
Guest Conductors	1927–1931
Albert van Raalte	1932–1933
John Barbirolli	1932–1933
John Barbirolli	1933–1936
George Szell	1936–1939
Aylmer Buesst	1939–1940
Warwick Braithwaite	1940–1945
Sir Thomas Beecham	1945
Walter Susskind	1946–1952
Karl Rankl	1952–1956
Hans Swarowsky	1957–1959
Alexander Gibson	1959 to date

10

MAIN EUROPEAN
AND AMERICAN ORCHESTRAS

LEIPZIG GEWANDHAUS ORCHESTRA

ALTHOUGH IT IS PERHAPS NOT THE BEST KNOWN ORCHES-
tra in Europe, and today this is partly because it lies in East
Germany, is one which counts first in the world in terms of
longevity and date of formation (1743). This is the Leipzig
Gewandhaus Orchestra. 'Gewandhaus' means 'Cloth Hall' because the first concert was held in the hall of the Leipzig linen
guild during J. S. Bach's appointment as Cantor of the St
Thomas's School. The first performance was held in a private
house under the conductorship of Herr Doles, a former pupil of
Bach, and consisted of only sixteen players. After the Seven
Years War was over, the concerts continued with an orchestra
augmented to thirty and entitled 'Liebhaberconcerte' or 'lovers'
concerts'. The concerts continued until 1778, when they trans-
ferred to the Gewandhaus, thanks to the support of the Burgomaster, Karl Wilhelm Müller, who may be considered as the
true founder of the concerts in their later form and of the insti-
tuion which is their corporate body. Müller and eleven other
Leipzig personalities formed the first board of directors and
appointed J. A. Hiller as the conductor. Due to the success of the
enterprise, the old Gewandhaus became far too small, and in
1884 a newly built concert hall was opened, with all possible
amenities for symphony concerts as well as a smaller hall for
chamber concerts. The institution continued to call itself by the
name Gewandhaus, although they had left that hall. The present
day orchestra has toured in the Western world, and has displayed its excellence. The principal conductors, since the
beginning, have been:

Johann Friedrich Doles	1743–1756
Johann Adam Hiller	1756–1778
Johann Adam Hiller	1781–1785
Johann Gottfried Schicht	1785–1810
J. C. P. Schulz	1810–1827
Christian August Pohlenz	1827–1835
Felix Mendelssohn	1835–1843
Ferdinand Hiller	1843–1844
Niels Gade	1844–1848
Julius Rietz	1848–1860
Karl Reinecke	1860–1895
Artur Nikisch	1895–1922
Wilhelm Furtwängler	1922–1930
Bruno Walter	1930–1933
Hermann Abendroth	1934–1945
Herbert Albrecht	1946–1948
Franz Konwitschny	1949–1962
Vaclav Neumann	1964–1968
Kurt Masur	1970 to date

Berlin Philharmonic Orchestra is not the oldest orchestra in Germany by any means, and not the oldest in Berlin either. The old court orchestras are known to have existed as early as 1574, but probably consisted mainly of amateurs. But the Berlin Philharmonic, now one of the most famous, and possibly the most accomplished in the world, is of relatively new foundation. It was brought into existence in 1882, in close association with the Berlin Singakademie. This important choral society, which was to be the model for all others in Germany, was founded in 1791, but deferred to the Berlin Philharmonic in 1907, by giving a celebratory silver jubilee concert in the Orchestra's honour. The orchestra was temporarily disbanded in 1944, but started up again a year later under Furtwängler as first conductor. Because he was abroad so much, Celibidache was named as the resident conductor. On Furtwängler's death, the conductorship passed to Herbert von Karajan who has made the orchestra 'the extension of my own right arm', as he affectionately puts it. Today it is a supreme instrument.

Principal conductors have been:

Karl Klindworth	1884–1897
Josef Rebiček	1897

Artur Nikisch	1897–1922
Wilhelm Furtwängler	1922–1934
Wilhelm Furtwängler	1935–1945
Sergiu Celibidache	1945
Wilhelm Furtwängler	1946–1954
Herbert von Karajan	1954 to date

Vienna Philharmonic Orchestra was formed from the Gesellschaft der Musikfreunde (which more or less means the same as Philharmonic Society). This Society was founded in 1813 and its orchestra was conducted by its members in rotation. They say, in Vienna, that the Orchestra really began its life in the Redoutensaal of the Imperial Palace under Otto Nicolai on 28 March 1842. By 1848, when Nicolai had already left them, they experienced serious difficulties, especially during the revolution. It was not until 1851 that the first established conductor arrived, and from then on they have been:

Joseph Hellmesberger	1851–1859
Johann Herbeck	1859–1870
Anton Rubenstein	1871–1872
Johannes Brahms	1872–1875
Johann Herbeck	1875–1877
Eduard Kremser	1878–1880
Wilhelm Gericke	1880–1884
Hans Richter	1885–1890
Wilhelm Gericke	1890–1895
R. von Perger	1895–1900
Friedrich Löwe	1900–1904
Franz von Schalk	1904–1908
Felix Weingartner	1908–1927
Wilhelm Furtwängler	1927–1930
Clemens Krauss ⎱ Richard Strauss ⎰	1930–1933
Guest conductors	1933–1938
Wilhelm Furtwängler	1938–1945
None*	1947–1954
Guest conductors	1954 to date

Concertgebouw Orchestra of Amsterdam. In 1883 the Concert-

* Furtwängler considered himself still to be the principal conductor and behaved as such until his death in 1954.

gebouw Society was formed (the word Concertgebouw meaning 'Concert Building') although its hall was not finished until 1888. The orchestra was raised by private subscription and the conductors have been these:

Willem Kes	1888–1895
Willem Mengelberg	1895–1938
Eduard van Beinum	1938–1945
Willem Mengelberg	1938–1945
Eduard van Beinum	1945–1959
Eugen Jochum	1961–1963
Bernard Haitink	1961–1963
Bernard Haitink	1964 to date

Boston Symphony Orchestra owes its existence, as well as its support for thirty-seven years, to the initial obsession, and later to the immense generosity of a Bostonian called Henry Lee Higginson. While in Vienna as a young man, he realised the standards achieved by European orchestras, and decided that he would not rest until he had founded 'an orchestra which should play the best music in the best way, and give concerts to all who could pay a small price' in America. Having returned home, he inserted an advertisement in the Boston newspaper which read:

The orchestra to number 60, and their remuneration to include the concerts and 'careful training'. Concerts to be 20 in number, on Saturday evenings, in the Music Hall, from middle of October to middle of March. Single tickets from 75 to 25 cents; season tickets (concerts only) 10 to 5 dollars; one public rehearsal 25 cents entrance.

The first concert duly took place as advertised on 22 October 1881.

Up to 1918, all deficits (and there were deficits for every season except one) were met by Higginson, but in that year the orchestra was incorporated, with a local judge as chairman of a board of ten trustees. Deficits are now met through income derived from an endowment fund. Since 1903 the orchestra has had its own pension fund, willingly subscribed by the members who, until after the last war, were non-union members, the only such orchestra in America. In 1900 the orchestra moved into Symphony Hall, where they have been ever since, while not touring in New England and New York. The 'Boston Pops' have been a finite part of the orchestra's activities since 1885, and have been given by a reduced force of players under Arthur Fiedler since 1930. The resident conductors of the Boston Symphony Orchestra have been:

George Henschel	1881–1884
Wilhelm Gericke	1884–1889
Artur Nikisch	1889–1893
Emil Paur	1893–1898
and	1898–1906
Karl Muck	1906–1908
Max Fiedler	1908–1912
Karl Muck	1912–1918
Henri Rabaud	1918–1919
Pierre Monteux	1919–1924
Serge Koussevitsky	1924–1949
Charles Munch	1949–1962
Erich Leinsdorf	1962–1969
William Steinberg	1969–1973
Seiji Ozawa	1973 to date

Chicago Symphony Orchestra is the third oldest orchestra in America, as they proudly boast, and began its life in 1891 as the Chicago Orchestra. There had been concerts in the city since 1864, and five years later a musical philanthropist called Theodore Thomas (leader of another orchestra) gave the first Thomas Concert there. Thomas left his itinerant orchestra in 1890 and founded the new one in 1891. Between 1909 and 1912 the name of the orchestra was changed to The Theodore Thomas Orchestra, but in 1912 the name was changed to, and has remained that of today. When Thomas died in 1905, his assistant became the resident conductor. The list of them is as follows:

Theodore Thomas	1891–1905
Frederick Stock	1905–1942
Desiré Defauw	1942–1947
Artur Rodzinski	1947–1948
Tauno Hannikainen	1948–1950
Rafael Kubelik	1950–1953
Fritz Reiner	1953–1963
Jean Martinon	1963–1968
Irwin Hoffman (acting)	1968–1969
Sir Georg Solti	1969 to date

Cincinnati Symphony Orchestra began in 1895, but the events that led up to this may be attributed to the efforts of Theodore Thomas (see under *Chicago SO*). In 1872 he was visiting Cincinnati as leader of a travelling orchestra, when the idea was put to him of organising an annual choral festival, sung in English, and with strong orchestral support. Thomas continued to conduct what was eventually to become a permanent, local choir that varied in size from 400–600 voices, until 1904. The Cincinnati Orchestra Association was formed in 1895 as a direct result of the formation of the Choir, and subsisted as the result of stockholdings and a debenture fund. Between 1907–1909 the orchestra voluntarily disbanded itself rather than suffer the dictates of the American Federation of Musicians (the Americans' Musicians' Union), but it was successfully reorganised under Leopold Stokowski. Its list of principal conductors is as follows:

Frank van der Stucken	1895–1896
Anton Seidl	1895–1896
Henry Schradieck	1895–1896
Frank van der Stucken	1896–1907
orchestra disbanded	1907–1909
Leopold Stokowski	1909–1912
Ernst Kunwald	1912–1917
Guest conductors	1917–1918
Eugène Ysaÿe	1918–1922
Fritz Reiner	1922–1931
Eugene Goossens Jr.	1931–1946
Thor Johnson	1947–1958
Max Rudolf	1958–1969
Erich Kunzel	1969–1970
Thomas Schippers	1970 to date

Cleveland Orchestra was launched in 1918 by the Cleveland Musical Arts Association, under the inspired initiative of Mrs Adella Prentiss Hughes, who was the orchestra's manager from its inception and until 1933. There is a large annual maintenance fund which provides for the orchestra's needs; and in 1929, due to the campaigning of Dudley S. Blossom, sufficient funds were raised to perpetuate an annual maintenance grant. Until 1931, concerts were given in the Masonic Hall, but in that year a local businessman called John L. Severance made a gift of a splendid new hall that bears his name, as a memorial to his wife. The conductors of this always well-endowed orchestra have been:

Nicolai Sokolov	1918–1933
Artur Rodzinski	1933–1946
George Szell	1946–1970
Lorin Maazcl	1972 to date

Philadelphia Orchestra came into being in November 1900 as a direct result of two concerts being given in the city that Spring by a new orchestra under Fritz Scheel, formerly an assistant to Bülow in Hamburg. This was the culmination of other efforts to form a permanent orchestra since Theodore Thomas had first inspired local citizens by his visits to them (see *Chicago SO*). The Philadelphia Orchestra Association sent Scheel abroad to recruit members for the permanent orchestra, and trained them into a firm instrument by the beginning of the season in the autumn of 1900. The present orchestra still owes a great deal to Stokowski, in matters of its ensemble. Its conductors have been:

Fritz Scheel	1900–1907
Karl Pohlig	1907–1912
Leopold Stokowski	1912–1941
Eugene Ormandy	1941 to date

NBC Symphony Orchestra was raised and trained in October 1937 by Artur Rodzinski as a broadcasting orchestra for Toscanini. Its concerts were broadcast from New York and simultaneously broadcast over many wavelengths in the United States. Its first broadcast concert was by Pierre Monteux in November 1937. and Toscanini was first heard on Christmas night a month later. He became the permanent conductor in the following year:

Arturo Toscanini	1938–1941
Leopold Stokowski and others	1941–1942
Arturo Toscanini	1942–7 April 1954

Although Toscanini occasionally returned to give guest performances after his official date of retirement in 1954, the orchestra was never the same; and when Toscanini died, it died too, despite valiant efforts on the part of its members.

New York Philharmonic Symphony Orchestra was an amalgamation of the Philharmonic Society and the New York Symphony Society, from both of which names the present one is drawn. Because the Philharmonic Society is so long established, and it is from its foundation that the present orchestra claims its origins, it is as well to start there. The Society was founded after a meeting of professional musicians in New York in April 1842, under the chairmanship of Ureli Corelli Hill. The first concert took place in the Apollo Rooms, New York on 7 December 1842. At first the Society adopted the normal custom of the times in giving the conductorship to the Society's president, but in fact it was shared. The principal conductors began to be appointed from 1852 and were as follows:

Theodore Eisfield	1852–1855
Theodore Eisfield	1855–1864
Carl Bergman	1855–1864
Carl Bergman	1865–1876
Three different conductors	1876–1878
Theodore Thomas	1879–1891
Anton Seidl	1891–1898
Emil Paur	1898–1902
Walter Damrosch	1902–1903
Guest conductors	1903–1906
Vassily Safonov	1906–1909
Gustav Mahler	1909–1911
Josef Stransky	1911–1921

At this point the amalgamation took place, but it is necessary to trace back for two years to when the New Symphony Orchestra was formed:

Edgar Varèse, the début:	11 April 1919
Artur Bodansky	1919–1920
Artur Bodansky	1920–1921
Willem Mengelberg	1920–1921

The orchestra was then renamed the National Symphony, and was merged with the Philharmonic Society in April 1921. Conductors were nominated jointly from both orchestras as follows:

Josef Stransky with
   Artur Bodansky and
   Willem Mengelberg as guests 1921–1922

Josef Stransky	1922–1923
Willem Mengelberg	1922–1923
Willem Mengelberg	1923–1924
Willem van Hoogstraten	1923–1924
Willem van Hoogstraten	1924–1925
Willem Mengelberg	1925–1927
Wilhelm Furtwängler	1925–1927
Arturo Toscanini	1926–1927
Arturo Toscanini	1927–1928
Willem Mengelberg	1927–1928
Arturo Toscanini	1928–1929
with Mengelberg & Molinari	1929–1930
Arturo Toscanini	1930–1936
interregnum	1936–1937
John Barbirolli	1937–1940
many changes of conductor	1940–1942
Artur Rodzinski	1942–1947
many changes of conductor	1947–1949
Leopold Stokowski	1949–1950
Dimitri Mitropoulos	1949–1950
Dimitri Mitropoulos	1950–1958
Leonard Bernstein	1958–1969
Bernstein as occasional 'Conductor Laureate'	1970–1971
Pierre Boulez	1971–1975

POSTSCRIPT

I DON'T THINK YOU WILL HAVE BEEN PUT OFF FROM JOIN-
ing an orchestra by the tone of this book! No musician who loves
music and loves playing would want to do any other job even if
he is not one hundred per cent content (and very few of us can
expect perfection in our chosen careers). All the same, it is in
the Arts where we come nearest to perfection, and a perfection
that is all the more satisfying because it is shared by others,
alongside you, and out in front. The achievement of being part
of a really outstanding performance of a great work and under a
great conductor is the kind of event that makes life really worth
living. Many players join the Covent Garden Orchestra for a
season just so that they can play in two *Ring* cycles under Kempe
or Solti or whoever it might be. This is experience with a
capital E, not merely playing experience but an uplifting and
totally consuming one.

So many of our music schools concentrate upon turning out
embryonic soloists, which is patently nonsensical. Real soloists
are of the genius squad, and being a genius is generally com-
pensated for in other directions which invariably make life difficult. So be grateful to be a normal player instead, it is far more
comfortable. And by the time you have gained your technique,
your life's die will be cast, and there can be no other career for
you, save in that necessary digression which I recommended in
my preface. By this time, no other profession will do, can be
even remotely considered. The training has been a long one, the
hours put in, immense. But you will have become a *musician*, an
active interpreter of the world's music, given only to the very
few. It is all very, very well worth while.

A.J.

APPENDICES

TRILINGUAL NAMES OF ORCHESTRAL INSTRUMENTS

English	German	Italian
Piccolo	kleine Flöte	Flauto piccolo
Flute	Flöte	Flauto
Oboe	Hoboe	Oboe
Cor anglais	englisches Horn	Corno inglese
E♭ Clarinet	Es-Klarinette	Clarinetto-mibemolle
D Clarinet	D-Klarinette	Clarinetto-re
B♭ Clarinet	B-Klarinette	Clarinetto-sibemolle
A Clarinet	A-Klarinette	Clarinetto-la
Basset-horn	Bassethorn	Corno di bassetto
Bass Clarinet	Bass Klarinette	Clarinetto basso
Saxophone	Saxophon	Saxofono
Bassoon	Fagott	Fagotto
Contra-bassoon	Kontrafagott	Contra fagotto
Horn	Horn	Corno
Trumpet	Trompete	Tromba
Cornet	Piston	Cornetta
Flugelhorn	Flugelhorn	Flicorno
Trombone	Posaune	Trombone
Tuba	Tuba	Tuba
Timpani	Pauken	Timpani
Bass Drum	grosse Tromell	Gran Cassa
Tenor Drum	Ruhrtrommel	Tamburo rullante
Side-drum	kleine Trommel	Tamburo militaire
Cymbals	Beckon	Piatti *or* Cinelli
Triangle	Triangel	Triangolo
Tambourine	Schellentrom	Tamburino
Gong	Tam-tam	Tam-tam
Glockenspiel	Glockenspiel	Campanetta
Xylophone	Xylophon	Zilafone
Celesta	Celeste	Celesta
Bells	Glocken	Campanelle
Harp	Harfe	Arpa
Violin	Violine	Violino
Viola	Bratsche	Alto
(Violon) cello	(Violon) cell	Violoncello
Double Bass	Kontrabass	Contrabasso

ORCHESTRAL LAYOUTS

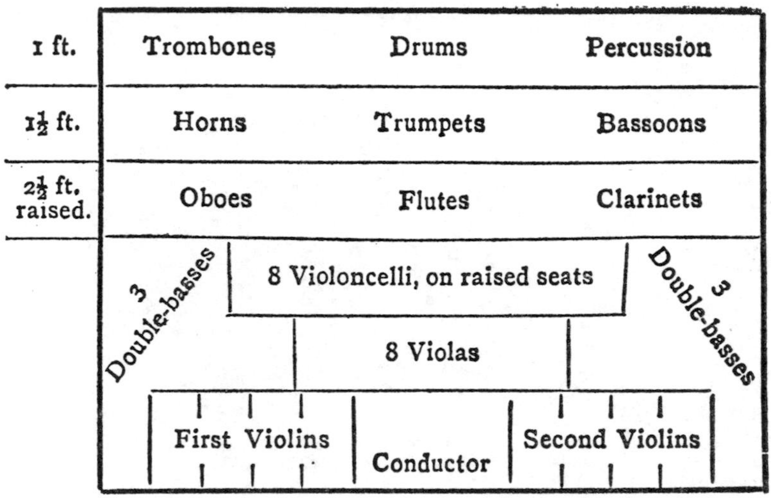

1 ft.
Trombones
Drums
Percussion
1½ ft.
Horns
Trumpets
Bassoons
2½ ft. raised.
Oboes
Flutes
Clarinets
3 Double-basses
8 Violoncelli, on raised seats
3 Double-basses
8 Violas
First Violins
Conductor
Second Violins

Fig. 11. Diagram of Wagner's layout of the orchestra in 1845

Kettle Drums
Double Basses
Tuba
Large Drum
Trombones
Triangle
Side Drum
Cornets
Double Basses
Horns
Bassoons
Oboes
Clarinets
Violas
Flutes
Violoncellos
First Violins
Second Violins
Harp
Conductor

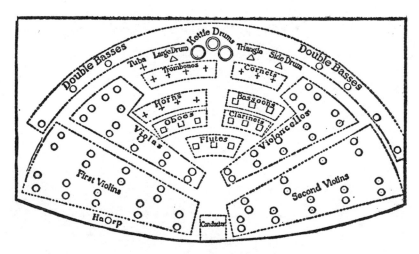

Fig. 12. Diagram showing layout of the New York Philharmonic Society Orchestra in 1897

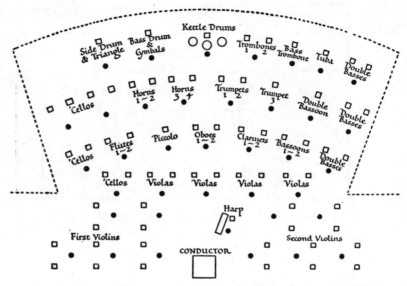

Fig. 13. *Diagram showing a frequent twentieth-century layout of the orchestra in London*
(*also see fig. 4 on p. 38 for another of 1784*)

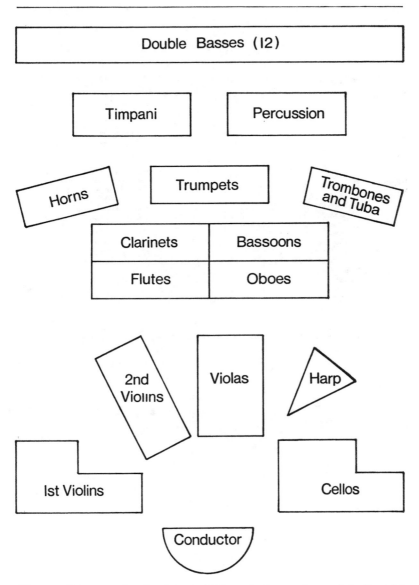

Fig. 14. Diagram showing layout of the orchestra as favoured by Leopold Stokowski

INSTRUMENTAL AND VOCAL COMPASSES

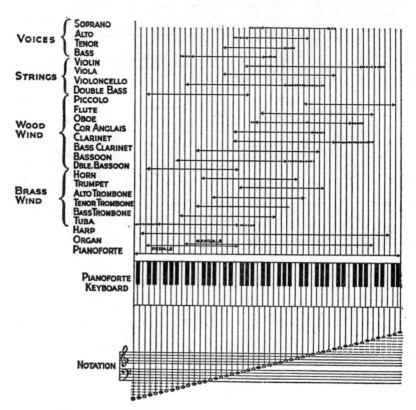

Fig. 15. *Diagram showing instrumental and vocal compasses*

GLOSSARY OF TERMS

A The sixth degree in the scale of C major, by which the orchestra all tune together. At 68°F this pitch was fixed, in 1813, as 439 cycles per second, but has since risen to 444 cps in common usage. The interval gong at the Royal Festival Hall in London sounds this note, and the oboe gives it out to the orchestra when there is no keyboard instrument on the platform. When there is one, tuning is from A above middle C on the piano, organ or harpsichord.

ACCIDENTALS The signs of ♯ and ♭ and ♮, which when placed before a note sharpens, flattens or reduces it respectively to the natural form. There is also X and ♭♭, meaning double sharp and double flat. These are required in the keys that already have several flats or sharps in the key signatures. The accidental sign pertains throughout the bar, as opposed to the signs as part of the key signature which follow throughout. Accidentals are temporary changes, often used to modulate from the home key.

ACOUSTICS A complicated and involved as well as an insecure science which has many imponderables. The reader is recommended to read it up first in an encyclopaedia before proceeding to a complete book on the subject.

ALTO The second 'voice' in a four-part harmony; the highest male voice. French and Italian for 'Viola', but this is a contradiction since in a string quartet the viola takes the third, or tenor, line.

ARPEGGIO A chord which has its notes spread in sequence, either up or down, and not played together.

ARPEGGIONE See p. 40.

BACK (desk implied).

BASS To string players this means the double bass. To woodwind players it means the bass clarinet, and to trombone and tuba players it means the bass tuba.

BELL The widest, open end of a wind instrument.

BELLS Usually tubular bells (see p. 81 and plate facing p. 11).

BRASS DEPARTMENT Consists of (horns) trumpets, trombones and tuba.

BRIDGE The piece of wood (in stringed instruments) which supports the strings in the raised position above the table, and transmits their vibrations to the belly of the instrument. Also a term used as *bridge passage* which connects the first and second subjects in sonata form.

BOW At first a convex-shaped piece of wood supporting several hundred strands of horsehair which could be tightened or loosened, and with which the strings of a stringed instrument were scraped. Later the bow became straight, and the science of bows and their application to the strings is a science in itself.

BUMPER An extra wind instrument, usually a horn or trumpet which 'bumps up' the sound at climaxes, but the player of which is more often used in strenuous works to give the principal a rest. He sits on the principal player's open side, away from the other members of the section.

CHAMBER ORCHESTRA A small orchestra able to play, in the seventeenth–nineteenth centuries, in a drawing room or *chambre*. The term is now applied to duos, trios, quartets, quintets, etc.

CASE The case in which an instrument is carried about or packed for travel—wooden in the latter case. Normally it is of canvas for a stringed instrument, or of fibre glass. Cases are made for a pair of violins. In every case there are places for one or two bows. Wind players often have improvised cases for their instruments, even despatch bags.

CELLO Short for *Violoncello*, this is the bass or fourth 'voice' in the string quartet, although not the 'bass' in an orchestra. See p. 38.

CLEFS Those normally in use are seen on the pages of scores, as on pages 25, 27, 52, 53 and 85. Soprano or G; Alto or C; Tenor (or C, uncommon); and Bass or F.

CHROMATIC Means literally 'coloured'. A chromatic passage or scale includes all the tones and semitones in the scale. So a chromatic chord will contain one or more notes not in the prevailing scale.

COLL' ARCO Italian for 'with the bow'. See p. 42.

COLOUR A transference of visual variety to music. See p. 44.

COMPASS The number of octaves and fractions of an octave which an instrument can play.

CONDUCTOR'S LEFT AND RIGHT Taken as he faces the orchestra.

COR French for 'Horn', but in musicians' parlance meaning the *cor anglais*, which is neither a horn, nor is it English. See p. 49.

DEPUTY A player engaged on (usually) a temporary basis to fill the position of a regular orchestral player who is absent.

DESK The arrangement of two chairs and one music stand at which two players sit, side by side, with the senior of the two on the side nearer to the audience. It applies exclusively to string players. One player sitting alone is called a 'half desk'.

DOWNBEAT When a conductor beats out the time of a composition, his stick (or hand) moves downwards for the first or 'strong' beat downbeat signifies that the session has begun. Not every work starts on the downbeat or first beat of the bar, and so the conductor may guide the players in with a preliminary or 'empty' beat or bar.

DYNAMICS The marks of expression in a score which indicate variations in speed, volume and other nuances.

EMBOUCHURE French for 'mouthpiece', but in normal parlance it applies to the positions of the lips to the mouthpiece of a wind instrument.

ENSEMBLE French for 'together'. In orchestral playing it signifies entire co-operation between all departments so as to achieve the proper balance required. As a group (Brass ensemble, wind ensemble) it means a group of players, usually one to a part.

FIDDLE Nickname for violin and viola. See pp. 33 and 35.

FUNDAMENTAL See diagram of the Harmonic Series on page 28. The bottom, bass G is the *fundamental* of the series.

'GIG' An independently arranged personal public appearance with an *ad hoc*, or other, group or orchestra.

GLISSANDO Dog-Italian from the French 'glisser' to slide. A rapid passing of the fingers along one string of a stringed instrument so that the sound comprises an infinite series of notes all run together to produce a seamless 'scale'. Also possible on the clarinet.

HALF DESK See *Desk*.

HAND-STOPPING (Horn) see p. 65.

HARMONIC SERIES See pp. 28–9.

HAUTBOIS Old French for *oboe*, and a name also used in mediaeval and Tudor England for the instrument, pronounced 'hort-boys'.

HORN Musicians always mean French horn, never *cor anglais*.

INSTRUMENTATION The number and variety of instruments which the composer has indicated in the score for each composition. See 'Anatomy of the Orchestra', pp. 22–28.

INTONATION The art of singing or playing in tune, completely in tune, 'in the middle of the note'.

LEADER The first player of the first violins who sits on the conductor's left, and who should be the most important and influential member of the orchestra. See pp. 31–32.

LEGER LINES Short lines, sufficient to indicate the position of a note above or below the normal stave. Middle C is the one leger line common to both treble and bass staves. The word can be spelt *Ledger*, but *Leger* is probably correct, emanating from the French word meaning 'light'.

MARKINGS Pencil notes added by orchestral players to their parts after instruction from the conductor. String players may also receive markings from their principals or the leader especially with regard to bowing.

MODULATION A change of key within a passage, effected easily and
usually pleasantly. For instance in the hymn tune, 'Onward Christian
Soldiers', there is a modulation into a closely related key with the
words '. . . Cross of Jesus' so that we are in another key for the
remainder of the line only. Modulation applies only to tonal compositions (*q.v.*)

MONO-CHORD A stringed instrument with only one string, as the
Trumpet Marine, see p. 69.

MUTE For stringed instruments this is a kind of clamp which is placed
on the bridge, thereby producing a different tone altogether, not
muted so much as mutated. For brass instruments it is a cone-shaped
piece of papier-maché (usually) that alters the sound produced by
diminishing it. Timpani players sometimes use a piece of cloth as a
mute, or soft-headed sticks. *Mute* does not mean 'silent' to players;
this word is *tacet* or *tacit* (*q.v.*).

NECK That part of a stringed instrument which projects from the sound-
box, carries the finger-board, and ends at the peg-box.

NOTE Properly, in acoustic terminology, note = sound + upper
partials. This fine description is not in general use.

OBOE, FIRST The player who sounds the A (*q.v.*) that draws all the
instruments of the orchestra to tune to him.

ON Really a stage term used by actors and, as a result, by everybody in
the entertainment business to describe the action of appearing in
front of the audience. 'Please go on' means, and implies '. . . to
the platform' to a musician. 'What time are we on?' means 'What
time does the concert start?'

ORCHESTRA From a Greek word meaning 'to dance' because the area
in front of the ancient Greek theatre, stage, where the chorus danced
and sang, was so called. The only similarity now exists at the opera
house, where the orchestra pit is in the same relative position,
although the singing and dancing goes on elsewhere (as a rule).
The common meaning of the word is now the band of musicians who
make up the body of players who create music, together with their
instruments.

ORCHESTRA, COMPASS OF THE From the lowest note of all on the tuba, to the highest note of all on the piccolo, and all those in between by all instruments involved.

OVERBLOW, TO To take the sound of the (wind) instrument into another octave. See p. 46.

PARTIALS, UPPER Another name for harmonics (q.v.).

PARTS Analysis from the full score of one (or a group, if the same music is played by every) instrument. Thus each desk or section has a different part, and when these parts are placed throughout the orchestra they represent the whole score spread out.

PEDAL NOTE The fundamental note (q.v.).

PEGS Wooden pegs at the top end of a stringed instrument, round which the strings are wound, and by adjustment of which the strings may be tightened (sharper) or loosened (flatter).

PERCUSSION That department of the orchestra whose instruments are all struck. See pp. 74–86.

PICCOLO Italian for 'little'. The smallest member of the Flute family.

PITCH, PERFECT Some people are able to sound or to sing any note to order, and to tell instantly when a note or a series of notes are not being played in the right key. Otherwise known as 'Absolute Pitch' it is both a boon and a curse to musicians. String players generally come quite near to acquiring it; but then to hear unmusical people mauling some celebrated tune, is most distressing, if not painful to the perfectly pitched listener.

PIZZICATO 'Plucked' (singular). *Pizzicati* (plural) *Pizz.* as the usual abbreviation. Applies only to string players who use one finger and not the bow.

PORTAMENTO Italian for 'carrying', and applies in vocal and bowed music where the tone is carried from one note to another without any noticeable gap between them. This is different from slurred notes or swooping phrases. *Portamento* can be artistic, and is meant to be.

PRINCIPAL Apart from the first violins, who have their Leader (q.v.), every other section has its *Principal*, who is the chief player there.

He may have a *Co-Principal* who alternates with him, or a *Sub-Principal* who is always there and is his second-in-command.

QUARTET The String Quartet is formed of two violins, one viola and one cello, and is the basic group of string players. It also applies to four of any instruments, including especially the Horns, and four voices: soprano, alto, tenor and bass.

RANK AND FILE Abbreviated to R/F, are the body of the string players of an orchestra, those who sit behind the first desks of violins, violas, cellos and double basses.

REED A thin piece of cane (in woodwind instruments) and sometimes also of metal, which beats after being breathed on or against, and so sets up sound in the instrument.

REPETITEUR In an orchestra this means the violin player who sits next to the Leader, although the term is in decline, being superseded by Sub-Leader, and occasionally by Co-Leader. In the opera house it has another meaning: that of a member of the musical staff who coaches the singers, and who may also prompt them in performance.

RIPIENO Italian for 'full'. In old music this signified what we now mean by *Tutti* = 'All', as opposed to a group of players who were called *Concertante*. In the brass band world, one comes across the word grossly (and always) misspelt as *ripiano* and *repiano*, referring to an instrument which (antithetically) plays only some of the time!

ROSTRUM A platform, from the Latin word for a 'beak', because that part of the prow of a Roman ship (beak-like) was called the *Rostrum* (plural *rostra*). *The rostrum* means the place where the conductor stands, also known as 'the stand' or 'the box'. But rostra are also used to elevate the brass and percussion players behind the rest so that they can see the conductor.

SCHOOLS OF MUSIC The principal schools in London are:
The Royal Academy of Music (1822)
The Royal College of Music (1882)
The Guildhall School of Music (1880)
Trinity College of Music (1875)
and outside London are:
The Royal Manchester College of Music (1893)
The Royal Scottish Academy of Music (1929)

The Royal School of Church Music (1927)
Royal Military School of Music (Kneller Hall) (1857)

SCORE (noun) The blueprint of a composition from which the parts
(*q.v.*) may be taken and the work played. The *full score* is in the
hands of the conductor. A *miniature score* is the same, photographed
or otherwise reduced down to handy size for the pocket; a *piano
score* is a reduction of all the orchestral parts for reproduction of the
work on a piano.
(verb) To *score* a work is to allot instruments to the composer's
already conceived ideas. Some composers are not able to score their
own works themselves, but this does not apply to living composers
and serious music. A sketch of a composition may be scored after a
composer's death by another hand, i.e. Deryck Cooke and Mahler's
Tenth Symphony.

SECONDS The Second Violins.

SEMITONE The smallest interval used in classical and romantic music,
but extended by Alois Hába and others who experimented in micro-
tones. Easily recognised semitones are from E to F, and from B to C;
and again between any black note on the piano and the white note
on either side of it.

SOPRANO Usually the highest singing voice. In the case of some brass
instruments it implies the highest type in its range, i.e. Soprano
Flügelhorn.

STAND See *Rostrum* above.

STEPPING-UP When a player is absent, the next senior—or chosen—
player is elevated to the vacant place, and so steps up. Depending on
the player's contract, and the situation, it may attract a higher fee or
payment.

STRAD, THE The string-player's 'trade paper'. The name is the normal
abbreviation of 'Stradivari', the celebrated Cremona family of violin-
makers from the mid-seventeenth to mid-eighteenth centuries.

STRING ORCHESTRA An orchestra with only stringed instruments
and no wind, brass or percussion.

STRINGS, THE The five string sections of an orchestra: the two violin sections (firsts and seconds), violas, cellos and double basses. (The Harp is counted as a percussion instrument).

SUB-LEADER See *Repetiteur* above.

SUB-PRINCIPAL See *Principal* above.

SYSTEM When there is room on a page of the score for more than one group of staves, the second group, known as a system, is printed below it and divided from the top system by two short black lines below the first bar.

TACET (sometimes spelt *Tacit*) Latin for 'he is silent'. Used ungrammatically by musicians: 'I'm tacet for the next five minutes, so there's just time for a pint'.

TECHNIQUE The mastery of any craft, after which the person can apply his mind to interpretation without the need for complete concentration upon the executive aspect.

TEMPO Italian for 'time' (singular). Plural *Tempi*. The speed chosen by the conductor for any work, and the variations of speed during it.

TENOR The second lowest part in a vocal quartet, hence, by implication, the Viola.

TIMPANI Italian for 'kettledrums' (plural). Never tympani, which are membranes.

TONE In acoustical language means simple vibrations without the upper partials.

TRANSPOSING INSTRUMENTS These are instruments which do not sound at the same pitch as indicated in the parts. See pp. 53–55.

UNISON Unity of pitch.

VOICES Not necessarily human voices, but 'strands' in a fugue, and thereby a melodic or other line in a composition.

WINDS Woodwind and Brass instruments.

SELECT READING LIST

There are, of course, too many books on music to be listed here, and such a catalogue would serve no useful purpose. The following titles, however, are especially relevant to the information in this book.

Bacharach, A. L. (Ed.), *Musical Companion*, London, Gollancz, 1940

Beecham, Sir Thomas, *A Mingled Chime*, London, Hutchinson, 1944

Elkin, Robert, *Queen's Hall*, London, Rider & Co., n.d.

Elkin, Robert, *Royal Philharmonic*, London, Rider & Co., n.d.

Groves' Dictionary of Music, London, Macmillan

Lambert, Constant, *Music Ho!* London, Faber, 1943

Scholes, Percy (Ed.), *Oxford Companion to Music*, London, OUP, 1942

Scholes, Percy (Ed.), *Concise Oxford Dictionary of Music*, London, OUP, 1952

Tobin, J. Raymond, *Music and the Orchestra*, London, Evans Bros. Ltd., 1961

INDEX

Key

comp	Composer
cond	Conductor
imp	Impresario
instr. mkr	Instrument Maker
mgr	Manager
mus	Musician
mus. crit	Music Critic
mus. pub	Music Publisher(s)
phil	Philanthropist
sop	Soprano
ten	Tenor

1. PERSONS

Adler, Larrie (Harmonica) 86
Amati (family) 16
Anderson, W. R. (mus. crit) 45
Arnold, Malcolm (comp)
  Ov: *Tam O'Shanter* 51
  Grand, Grand Overture 81

Bach, J. S. (comp) 60, 64, 98, 107, 152
Bacharach, A. L. (author) 45
Barbirolli, Sir John (cond) 149, 150, 151, 160
Barenboim, Daniel (cond/pianist) 94
Beecham, Sir Thomas (cond/imp) 61, 98–9, 100, 107, 108, 110, 143, 144, 145, 146, 147, 148, 151
Beethoven, L. van (comp) 24, 67, 96, 98, 104, 107, 109, 132, 141
  Symph. 5 52
      6 77, 111, 137
      7 32, 48
      9 52, 100, 142

Triple Concerto 39
Fidelio 52
Beinum, Eduard van (cond) 145, 155
Berlioz, Hector (comp)
  Damnation of Faust 71
  Symphonie Fantastique 57, 81, 83
  Treatise on Orchestration 74
Bernstein, Leonard (comp/cond) 20, 96, 160
Blossom, Dudley S. 157
Boehm, Theobald (flautist) 47
Boosey & Hawkes (mus. pub) 35
Boulez, Pierre (comp/cond) 59, 81, 137, 138, 141, 160
Boult, Sir Adrian (cond) 135–6, 143, 145, 150
Brahms, Johannes (comp) 24, 141, 154
  (cond) 75
  Academic Festival Ov: 75, 76
  Symph. 1 35
      4 75
  Second Serenade, 37
  Double Con. 39

Brain, Dennis (horn player) 65
Bravington, Eric (mgr) 109
Britten, Benjamin (comp)
  Serenade 66
Bruckner, Anton (cond) 23, 132
Brymer, Jack (clarinettist) 59, 137
Bülow, Hans von (cond) 75, 158
Busch, Fritz (cond) 84

Cameron, Basil (cond) 139
Cantelli, Guido (cond) 107, 146
Celibidache, Sergiu (cond) 153, 154
Chamberlain, Neville (politician) 149
Chappells, Messrs. (mus. pub) 147
Churchill, Winston S. (politician) 101
Civil, Alan (horn player) 138
Coates, Eric (comp)
  Rhapsody for Sax. 58
Cooke, Deryck (comp) 174
Cooper, Gary (actor) 72
Corri, P. A. (mus) 142
Cramer, J. B. (mus) 142

Dance, William (mus) 142
Davis, Colin (cond) 97, 137
Debussy, Claude (comp)
  Rhapsody for Sax. 58
Delius, Frederick (comp)
  1st. Dance Rhapsody 32, 60
  Double Con. 39
  Requiem 60
  Magic Fountain 126–7
Donizetti, Gaetano (comp)
  L'Elisir d'Amore 51
Dragonetti, Domenico (string bass player) 42
Dukas, Paul (comp)
  L'Apprenti Sorcier 51
Durbin, Deanna (sop) 98

Elgar, Sir Edward (comp/cond) 141, 143, 149
Elizabeth, Queen 101
Ellis, Osian (harpist) 83

Fauré, Gabriel (comp)
  Requiem 36
Fiedler, Arthur (cond) 155
Fischer, Edwin (pianist) 94
Flcischmann, Ernest (mgr) 145
Forsyth, Cecil (mus. crit) 78
Furtwängler, Wilhelm (cond) 143, 153, 154, 160

George, VI, King 101
Gershwin, George (comp) 20
  Rhapsody in Blue 56
Gilbert, W. S. see Sullivan, Sir A.
Giulini, Carlo Maria (cond) 146
Glock, Sir William (BBC Controller) 136, 141
Gluck, C. W. (comp) 49
  Orpheus 47
Godfrey, Sir Dan (cond) 148
Goodall, Reginald (cond) 96
Grétry, A. E. M. (comp)
  Zémire et Azor 98
Grieg, Edvard (comp)
  Piano Con. 77
Grove, Sir G. (ed.) 35
Groves, Sir Charles (cond) 148, 149

Hába, Alois (comp) 174
Haitink, Bernard (cond) 145, 155
Hall, Peter (producer) 147
Hallé, Sir Charles (cond/imp) 148
Hampl, (horn player) 65
Handel, G. F. (comp)
  'Gods go a-begging' arr. Beecham 98
  'Great Elopement' arr. Beecham 98
Harty, Sir Hamilton (cond) 143, 148
Haydn, Joseph (comp) 24, 67, 107, 141
Heckel, Wilhelm (instr. mkr) 60
Henze, Hans Werner (comp) 41
Heseltine, Philip (comp) 6
Higginson, Henry Lee (phil) 155
Hill, Uri Corelli (mus) 159
Hindemith, Paul (comp) 35

Hitler, Adolf (dictator) 107
Hoffnung, Gerard (artist) 45–6, 81
Holbrooke, J. (comp)
  Apollo and the Seaman 61
Holliger, Heinz (oboist) 49
Holst, Gustav (comp) 20
Hughes, Mrs. A. P. (phil) 157

Karajan, Herbert von (cond) 96, 103, 107, 146, 153, 154
Karr, Gary (string bass player) 41, 42
Kastner, J. G. (comp)
  Last King of Judah 58
Kempe, Rudolf (cond) 108, 146, 161
Kertesz, Istvan (cond) 145
Kes, Willem (cond) 150, 155
Klemperer, Otto (cond) 95–6, 97, 103, 107, 137, 146
Knappertsbusch, Hans (cond) 96
Koussevitsky, Serge (cond) 127, 156
Krips, Josef (cond) 145
Kubelik, Jan (violinist) 147

Lambert, Constant (comp)
  Rio Grande 77
Legge, Walter (imp) 107, 108, 110, 145, 146
Liszt, Franz (comp)
  Piano Con. 1 80

Maazel, Lorin (cond) 146, 158
Mahler, Gustav (comp/cond) 6, 23, 96, 132, 159
  10th. Symph. 174
Matthews, Appleby (cond) 149, 150
Melchior, Lauritz (ten) 94
Mendelssohn, Felix (comp)
  Ov: *Midsummer Night's Dream* 51
  (cond) 143, 153
Menuhin, Yehudi (violinist) 37
Monteux, Pierre (cond) 144, 145, 156, 158

Moody & Sankey (arrangers) 86
Mozart, Leopold (comp) 34
Mozart, Wolfgang (comp) 24, 67, 96, 107, 141
  Symph. 40 57
  Bassoon Con. 51
  Clarinet Con. 57
  Clarinet Quintet 57
  Flute & Harp Con. 83
  Requiem Mass 58, 70–1
  Don Giovanni 64, 97, 137
Müller, Karl Wilhelm (Burgomaster) 152
Mussorgsky, Modeste (comp)
  Boris Godunov 82

Newman, Robert (mgr) 147
Nicolai, Otto (cond) 154

Ormandy, Eugene (cond) 97, 158

Peyer, Gervase de (clarinettist) 59
Ponsonby, Robert (BBC Controller) 141
Previn, André (cond) 97, 145
Prokofiev, Serge (comp)
  Peter and the Wolf 51, 56

Reilly, Tommy (harmonica player) 86
Richter, Hans (cond) 145, 148
Rimsky-Korsakov, Nicholas (comp)
  Capriccio Espagnol 78
Ronald, Sir Landon (cond) 143, 144, 147, 150
Rossini, Gioacchino (comp)
  Ov: *La Gazza Ladra* 78
  Variations on *Mosé* 41
  Ov: *William Tell* 49, 119
Roth, Ernst (mus. pub) 141

Saint-Saëns, Camille (comp)
  Carnival of Animals 41
  Danse Macabre 82
Sargent, Sir Malcolm (cond) 100–1, 136, 137, 143, 148, 149
Sarrus (bandmaster) 61
Sax, Adolphe (instr. mkr) 58

Schnabel, Artur (pianist) 136
Schubert, Franz (comp)
  Arpeggione Sonata 40–1
Schumann, Robert (comp)
  Piano Con. 77
Severance, John I. (phil) 157–8
Shaw, G. B. (mus. crit) 58
Sibelius, Jan (comp)
  Swan of Tuonela 49
Solti, Sir Georg (cond) 88, 137,
  156, 161
Staufer, G. (instr. mkr) 40
Stokowski, Leopold (cond) 26–7,
  98, 157, 158, 160, 165
Stradivari (family) 174
Strauss, Richard (comp) 24, 60,
  72, 96
  (as instrumentalist) 75
  Also sprach Zarathustra 84
  Alpine Symphony 80
  Festival Prelude 84
  Heldenleben 31
  Symphonia Domestica 58, 59–60
  Till Eulenspiegel 57, 80
  Ariadne auf Naxos 21, 26, 27,
  84, 85
  Elektra 60
  Josephslegende 60
  Intermezzo 21
  Rosenkavalier 83
  Salome 60
Stravinsky, Igor (comp) 98
  Firebird 20
  Noces, Les 20
  Petrouchka 20, 72, 77, 78
Stuyvesant, Peter (phil) 108
Sullivan, Sir Arthur (comp)
  operas of 100–1
  (cond) 143
Suzuki, Mr (teacher) 36
Szell, George (cond) 95, 103, 150,
  151, 158

Tchaikovsky, Peter I. (comp)

Symph. 4 42
Symph. 6 79, 98
Piano Con. 1 77
Casse Noisette 83
Swan Lake 83
Hamlet Ov. Fantasie 79
'1812' Ov. 78
Tertis, Lionel (violist) 37
Thibouville-Lamy (instr. mkr) 34
Thomas, Theodore (phil. & cond)
  156, 157, 158, 159
Tomlinson, Ernest (comp)
  Con. for 4 Sax's 58
Torch, Sidney (comp) 73
  London Transport Suite 72
Toscanini, Arturo (cond) 78, 94–5,
  107, 127, 136, 158, 160

Vaughan Williams, Ralph (comp)
  Harmonica Concerto 86
  Job 58
  Sinfonia Antartica 81
Verdi, Giuseppe (comp)
  Requiem Mass 78
  Trovatore, Il 79

Wagner, Richard (comp) 59, 70,
  96
  (cond) 143, 163
  Lohengrin 71
  Ring, Der 71, 72, 161
  Das Rheingold 79
  Tannhäuser 94
Walton, Bernard (clarinettist) 59
Walton, Sir William (comp)
  Belshazzar's Feast 84
  Troilus and Cressida 101
Weber, Carl Maria von (comp)
  Bassoon 'Con' 51
Webster, Sir David (mgr) 101
Wills Ltd., W. D. & H. O. (phil)
  108
Wood, Sir Henry J (cond) 95,
  135, 143, 144, 147

2. ASSOCIATIONS, BOARDS, CONCERTS, FESTIVALS,
HALLS, ETC., ORCHESTRAS, SCHOOLS, SOCIETIES

ASSOCIATION, Cincinnati Orches-
tral 157
Cleveland Music Arts 157
Philadelphia Orchestra 158
BOARD, London Orchestral Con-
certs 107, 108, 109, 144
CONCERTS
Boston 'Pops' 155
Promenade ('Proms') 97, 100,
136, 137
Sir Robert Mayer's Children's
144
COUNCIL, Arts 108, 109, 150
Scottish Arts 150
FESTIVAL, Edinburgh 100
Glyndebourne 145
London Music 136

HALLS etc. (C) = Concert; (B) =
Broadcasting Studio; (R) = Re-
cording Studio; (O) = Opera
House
Austria, Vienna, Redoutensaal (C)
154
England, London, Aeolian Hall (B)
135
Argyll Rooms (C) 142
Barbican (C) 109
Crystal Palace (C) 92
Kingsway Hall (R) 40
Maida Vale (B) 135, 136
Paris 'Cinema' (B) 135
Playhouse (B) 135
Queen's Hall (C) 29, 135,
136, 144, 147
Royal Albert Hall (C) 109,
125, 136, 147
Royal Festival Hall (C) 15–
16, 45, 76, 109, 125, 139, 140
Royal Opera House, Covent
Garden (O) 52, 81, 97, 101,
137, 145
Sadler's Wells (O) 97, 137
Croydon, Fairfield Halls (C)
109, 125

Glyndebourne (O) 84, 145
Liverpool Philharmonic Hall (C)
149
Germany, Bayreuth (O) 94, 96
Leipzig Gewandhaus (C) 152
Netherlands, Amsterdam Concert-
gebouw (C) 154
USA, Boston Music Hall (O) 155
Symphony Hall (O) 155
Cleveland Masonic Hall (O)
157
Severance Hall (O) 158
New York Apollo Rooms (O)
159
Metropolitan (O) 96, 137

ORCHESTRAS
Austria, Vienna Philharmonic 154
England, BBC Symphony 97, 109,
135–41, 144, 147
BBC Orchestras (others) 104,
112, 140–1, 148
Beecham O. 107
Bournemouth Symphony 148
Sinfonietta 148
City of Birmingham Symphony
149
Covent Garden O. 161
English Chamber O. 146
English Sinfonia 146
Gentlemen's O, Manchester 148
Hallé 141, 148–9
London Mozart Players 146
Philharmonic O. 107, 108,
110, 145–6
Symphony O. 81, 97, 108,
110, 114, 129, 138, 139, 142,
144–5
Sinfonietta 146
New Philharmonia O. 108, 110,
138, 139, 145–6
New Queen's Hall O. 146–7
New Symphony O. 147
Philharmonia O. 107, 108, 110,
145–6

Royal Albert Hall O. 147
Royal Liverpool Philharmonic
    O. 149
Royal Philharmonic O. 107, 108,
    110, 139, 144, 146
Royal Philharmonic Society O.
    142–4
Germany, Berlin Philharmonic 76,
    107, 117
Leipzig Gewandhaus O. 142,
    152
Netherlands, Concertgebouw of
    Amsterdam 150, 154–5
Scotland, Scottish National O. 105,
    150
Scottish O. 150
USA, Boston Symphony O. 127,
    155–6
Chicago Symphony O. 156
Cincinnati Symphony O. 156–7
Cleveland O. 103, 157–8
NBC Symphony O. 94, 158
New York Philharmonic Sym-
    phony O. 96, 159–60
Philadelphia O. 97, 158

SCHOOLS OF MUSIC
England, Guildhall School of Music
    173

Royal Academy of Music 30,
    36, 173
Royal College of Music 30, 36,
    173
Royal School of Church Music
    174
Royal Military School of Music
    (Kneller Hall) 174
Royal Northern College of Music
    173
Trinity College of Music 173
Dartington Hall (Devon) 136
Germany, St. Thomas's School
    (Leipzig) 152
Japan, Suzuki School 36
Scotland, Royal Scottish Academy
    of Music 173

SOCIETIES
Austria, Vienna Gesellschaft der
    Musikfreunde 154
England, Liverpool, Royal Phil-
    harmonic S. of 149
London Orchestral Concert S.
    144
Royal Philharmonic S. 142–4
USA, New York Philharmonic S.
    159, 163
Symphony S. 159